CONTENTS

LIST OF MAPS DRAWN:

ACKNOWLEDGEMENTS

I wish to thank the large numbers of people who have provided help, information, advice, tea and sympathy in the preparation of this book. The staff of the Imperial War Museum have been very helpful, as have many county record offices. A number of regimental museums have supplied information for which I am grateful and special thanks go to the curator of the Northumberland Fusiliers for providing assistance and records.

Thanks also to Dennis Poulter of Sawston for the information on the Cambridgeshires and Corporal Jones. The staff of the Royal Engineers Corps Library have, as ever, been most kind and generous with their time, as have those at Saffron Walden public library. The people of Messines, especially those working at its church and museum, that I have met on field trips have all been courteous and helpful; Laurie Farrow of the Rijkswacht or Gendarmerie provided some valuable local information for which I am very grateful. John and Chris at the Shell Hole in Ypres have been hospitable, providing accommodation and hangovers. Lastly, many thanks to J.G. for endless support and patience.

Late 1916: a German priest holds Mass in a trench. German soldiers from Prussia and Baden had the motto 'Gott mit uns' on their belt; The British thought they also had God with them.

Battleground Europe

MESSINES RIDGE

Battleground Europe

MESSINES RIDGE

Peter Oldham

Series editor
Nigel Cave

LEO COOPER

First published in 1998 by
LEO COOPER
an imprint of
Pen Sword Books Limited
47 Church Street, Barnsley, South Yorkshire S70 2AS

ISBN 0 85052 624 8

A CIP catalogue of this book is available
from the British Library

Printed by Redwood Books Limited
Trowbridge, Wiltshire

*For up-to-date information on other titles produced under the Leo Cooper imprint,
please telephone or write to:*

Pen & Sword Books Ltd, FREEPOST, 47 Church Street
Barnsley, South Yorkshire S70 2AS
Telephone 01226 734222

Cover painting: **London Scottish on Messines Ridge during the night of 31 October,
1914** *by Caton Woodville.*
Courtesy of the Curator, London Scottish Regimental Museum.

INTRODUCTION BY SERIES EDITOR

Peter Oldham's previous book in this series took the reader to the relatively neglected area of the Hindenburg Line, where British cars have been few and far between, especially when compared to the considerable numbers that descend upon the battlefield of the Somme. The cars are, by comparison, plentiful on the road over the Messines Ridge, but few stop to look and see and fewer still have much concept of the scale of the fighting that took place along and below it between November 1914 and October 1918. This book serves to fill that gap effectively and with style.

The British battles of the Great War, with notable exceptions, have not been well served by military historians. Still awaited, for example, are detailed studies of Loos, Neuve Chapelle, Second Ypres - the list is considerable. It has always surprised me that the Battle of Messines, 7 - 14 June 1917, is amongst those still awaiting a full examination.

Messines was the first great set-piece action of British arms that resulted in complete victory - a victory in the air, underground, in artillery, in logistics and on the ground with the infantry. No full account, apart from that in the Official History, 1917, Volume II, has ever appeared. What makes this even more incomprehensible is that the area over which the battle was fought is easily accessible and there are considerable vestiges of the war, not least the large number of mine craters which are the product of the earth shattering blasts that accompanied the opening of the attack.

Therefore, although the book does not set out to be a detailed account of the battle, its description of the ground and the remnants of the war is combined with a coherent account of the fighting that took place here over those ghastly years of war, before the region was restored to its peaceful, agrarian nature. Peter Oldham brings to bear his vast knowledge of the ground and of the development and construction of the numerous pill boxes and larger concrete fortifications that were a characteristic of this part of the front. He has thereby done a great service to the rising number of pilgrims and visitors to this ridge, so important to the Ypres Salient, adjacent to the north. Perhaps a greater service has been done to those units and formations that fought under the command of 'Daddy' Plumer's Second Army, men whose achievements have thus far gone so unrecognised, at least in print.

Nigel Cave,
Ely Place, London

INTRODUCTION

Messines Ridge gained some fame following the 1917 battle for its possession. The villages on the ridge: Messines, Wytschaete and St. Eloi, also had battles raging within and around them throughout most of the Great War, the front line trenches were never far from the dwellings and all the buildings of all three were gradually reduced to dusty rubble by repeated shelling. St. Eloi, stuck onto the northern extremity of the ridge, actually had the British trenches running through the streets and under the houses, whilst Messines and Wytschaete were turned into fortified strongholds by the Germans. The reason was because of the view from the high ground over the Flemish plains to the west and the north, particularly towards Ypres, where the British were locked into the Salient.

From the crest of the ridge, along which runs the Armentières-Ypres road, the land slopes gently down to the east, beyond Houthem and Hollebeke to the Comines Canal with the parallel railway line on a high embankment. The canal is not used and, except for a few small ponds and reed beds at intervals along its length, it is a dry cutting overgrown with thick shrubbery and dense thickets. On the western side of the ridge the land falls sharply, especially at Messines, and this steep slope was used as a defence in earlier centuries. The River Douve, 1-2 metres wide, depending on the season, and in a deep

Sappers digging a forward communication trench during the battle of Messines Ridge.

cutting which makes crossing difficult, marks the southern end. The northern end of the ridge before the war contained many mature woods; many of these have either disappeared or reduced in size although some, notably Wytschaete Wood, Grand Bois and Petit Bois, have been retained. This area is renowned for the song of the nightingale and even during the war these birds were heard to sing melodiously in the devastated woodland. The land is still extensively farmed, which has resulted in many small copses and hedges being cleared to enlarge the size of fields, and makes the character of the landscape more bleak and exposed.

Messines village (some of its residents prefer it to be called a town) has a history dating back to Roman times. The Abbey (completely destroyed by shell fire and not rebuilt after the war) was founded by Countess Adela of France, who died there in AD1079 and whose tomb was in the crypt, which was replaced there in 1980. It is a pleasant village with a small square and a church which is clearly visible over most of the surrounding land, making a good navigational aid. The church and its crypt can be visited; the guide, Albert Gherkière, is pleased to give a full history. A contribution to the church bells, which were re-hung in 1986, is welcomed. Messines has a small but interesting museum on the market square, which has much information on the fighting around the village and a wealth of artefacts and historical pieces. The Museum Secretary, Patrick Colson, has considerable documentary information on the men from New Zealand who took the ruins in 1917.

Wytschaete, known as 'Whitesheet' to the British during the war, is larger but has the advantage of being set back off the main road which helps keep it a quieter place. It too has a large church which was used as a shelter, but visitors are not encouraged unless for religious purposes. St. Eloi, originally a hamlet at a road junction, has changed little from its pre-war size and layout although the placing there of a large roundabout a few years ago did make some difference.

Messines Ridge was in the early days of the war in the area opposite V Corps of the Second Army. The corps commander, General Herbert Plumer, was later to take overall control of the Second Army and was to mastermind the 1917 offensive that saw the Germans pushed off during the operation which became accepted as a masterpiece of planning and execution. Plumer (often referred to by historians and soldiers as 'Daddy' Plumer because of his reported concern for troops welfare, and also known as 'Old Plum and Apple' or 'Bottlenose' by the troops) was later to be given the accolade of Field-Marshal Viscount Plumer of Messines. The loser of that battle, General von Laffert, was not praised, he was sacked.

General Herbert Plumer

The intention of this book is to provide the battlefield visitor or armchair reader with a brief history of the events which occurred here between late October 1914 and the end of September 1918: four years of siege warfare over a handful of square kilometres. The battles and operations which flared up were later given official names and periods by the Battlefield Nomenclature Committee:

1914 The Battle of Messines, 10th October-2nd November.
       Attack on Wytschaete, 14th December.
1915 Action of St. Eloi, 14th-15th March.
1916 Actions of St. Eloi Craters, 27th March-16th April.
1917 Battle of Messines, 7th-14th June.
1918 Battle of Messines, 10th-11th April.
       Final Advance, 28th September-11th November.

The 1917 Battle of Messines, known as the 'Magnum Opus' to many of its planners and participants, is by far the most written about and famous of the actions. However all the other battles, and the 'quiet' periods in between when men of both sides lived like mud mites and died from shell fire, gas, sniper and machine gun fire, are periods in history which deserve not to be forgotten.

Today's visitor to the battleground of Messines Ridge will, at first sight, see little to tell of the events which happened there. There are two exceptions to this apparent lack of vestiges; the mine craters, which are large enough to warrant road diversions in some places, and some concrete monoliths, pill boxes which stand in farmers' fields or by the roadside, most showing signs of damage from the times they were hit by shelling or when the occupants were ousted. Due to the needs of agriculture the trenches, barricades, dugouts, and shell holes have all been flattened and ploughed over. Some of the woods show a similar lack of remnants of war, having been themselves dug up and replanted for timber. One of the woods, Croonart Wood, was kept in its immediate post-war state as a museum but this has now closed.

The aim of this book is to tell the story of Messines Ridge and the land and the three villages which comprise it: Messines, Wytschaete and St. Eloi. The hamlets of Oosttaverne, Wambeke and Gapaard appear on maps but can be difficult to identify as they consist of a few houses thinly spread along the N336. It lists what remains today to be seen of the of the battles and gives some guidance on what happened where and when. The 1917 Battle of Messines extended further north, the attacks by the left brigade of the 47th Division and the 23rd Division, north of the canal, took in The Bluff and Hill 60, these places are not covered but are worthy of books in their own right.

The spelling of Flemish place names is rarely consistent and varies from source to source, especially as some show French influence because of its closeness to the border. Messines is properly known as

Soldiers in a British communications trench near Ploegsteert Wood, 11 June 1917. These troops are waiting to go foward to relieve those in the front line at Messines. TAYLOR LIBRARY

Mesen, Wytschaete has several spellings (modern Belgian maps use Wijtschate) and St. Eloi can be St. Elois or St. Elooi. For this book the spellings adopted by the British Official History of the War have been used. Croonart Wood, named after the chapel which stood nearby, was sometimes called Bois Quarante, following the French who named it so because the 40 metre contour line runs through it. Road numbers can also confuse; the N365 is on some maps as the N69 and the N336 appears as the N65. One useful facet of Belgian roads is the road distance marker system, where each tenth of a kilometre is marked with a small white post.

There are now no hotels or other accommodation in the area covered by this book. The industrial town of Armentières has hotels but Ypres is closer, is more attuned to battlefield visitors, and is the centre of the tourist industry. Of the several hotels most are satisfactory; The Shell Hole, which also has a shop selling First World War books, souvenirs and memorabilia is recommended. Many battles have been analysed and replayed, and campaigns won over a Belgian beer in the bar. The large town square, the Grote Markt, has a number of restaurants and food and chocolate shops.

The people of Flanders are, on the whole, welcoming to visitors and many speak English but do not appreciate attempts at French as they prefer their own Flemish identity. Farmers are generally tolerant of people on their land provided that obvious courtesies with crops and livestock are adhered to.

Good maps are an essential piece of kit for any visitor. The maps in this volume should give some assistance in showing the location of the events covered, but for touring the area and general navigational purposes a good road atlas is advised. The Michelin 1:200000 series is easily available, widely used and very helpful: the French I.G.N. (Institute Geographique National) maps give greater detail but can be difficult to obtain. The new tourist office in Ypres has a full selection of maps.

MAP LEGEND

———	MAIN ROAD
——	LOCAL ROAD OR TRACK
▬▬	RAILWAY LINE
═══	CANAL
■	CEMETERY
△	MEMORIAL
●	GERMAN BUNKER
○	BRITISH BUNKER
✳	1915 MINE CRATER
❋	1916 MINE CRATER
✳	1917 MINE CRATER
▲	WINDMILL (pre-war)

Chapter One

1914. PUSHED OFF THE HILL

Towards the end of October 1914 the professional Regular soldiers of the British Army were slowly being pushed back towards the coast ports by the seemingly inexhaustable numbers of German troops. The battles of Mons and Le Cateau in August, followed by those of the Marne and the Aisne in September, resulted in reduced regiments of weary and footsore infantrymen and unmounted cavalry holding positions against repeated German attacks. Mobile cavalry units and field gun batteries were moved around the field as the hierarchy of both sides had expected and were used to. Since the first British troops landed in France on 14 August and encountered the Germans on the morning of 22 August the battles had been fought along familiar lines; the British using their experiences of fighting around the Empire and South Africa, and the Germans using skills aquired during continental scraps. But now the mobility had gone, trench positions were being established and soldiers and artillery were digging in for determined defence. The Germans, having pushed back the British, Belgians and French, were still intent on reaching the French coast to cut off the British lines at Calais and Boulogne, the British wanted to push northeastwards further into Belgium to out-flank them.

The fighting for Messines Ridge began in earnest on 21 October. The British held the ground well to the east of Messines village: the Cavalry Corps, comprising 1st Cavalry Division on the eastern slopes and the 2nd Cavalry Division in Kortewilde and Houthem. Three German cavalry divisions, the 4th, 9th and Guard, tried to press the British back through Messines and off the ridge but were unable to make any ground. The Bavarian and 6th Cavalry Divisions, after a heavy bombardment with field guns, drove the British cavalrymen out of their rudimentary trenches and back towards Hollebeke. A communications error resulted in the British troops then vacating Hollebeke Chateau and village, ready to fall back to St. Eloi; on receiving instructions to retake the ground lost they recaptured Hollebeke village – where the Germans had not taken advantage of the withdrawal, unaware of the extent of the retreat – but the Germans remained in control around the Chateau.

Orders were issued for the British cavalrymen to dig in and prepare defences for a further attempt by the Germans to push them off the

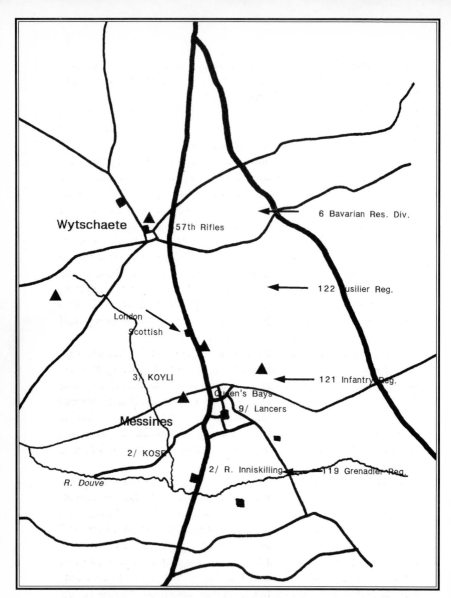

The attacks by the Germans on the British holding the eastern slopes of
the ridge during the last days of October 1914, and the British
reinforcements at Messines. Trenches at this stage were shallow and
rudimentary as they were thought to be temporary. Forward defences
were generally made by troops with the assistance of the Royal Engineers;
second line trenches were organised by 1st and 2nd Field Squadrons
Royal Engineers, who were attached to the Cavalry. The British were
slowly pushed westwards to the crest of the ridge, where the main road
runs, by the Germans through sheer weight of numbers. Once it was
apparent that the ridge was lost the British decided to fall back and cede
it to the attackers.

ridge. Trench lines were not continuous but disconnected shallow scrapings made, often under fire, with the limited number of tools to hand. Reinforcements were brought up where available. Indian cavalry of the Ferozepore Brigade and the 129th Baluchis, with the 9th Bhopal Infantry arrived, together with the 2nd Essex and then the 1st Connaught Rangers, who arrived by bus. The Germans made repeated attempts on the British lines, any small gains made were lost again and fighting was hard and severe as both sides tried to carry out orders, the Germans to move forward and the British to stay put. The German attacks include the use of mobile machine guns, fixed on motor cars, but the innovation was not successful and they were driven off. Artillery of both sides were very busy, with field guns being used to such a degree that mechanisms failed. The 2nd Essex, after recapturing a trench at Wambeke crossroads, reported an occurence which was to be reported again on the ridge two years later – finding three Germans, an officer, company sergeant-major and signaller, in a house, all dead but with no marks on them. The effects of concussion from heavy shell fire were to become much more common.

The Germans had numerical superiority over the British, and kept up the pressure on the defenders, whose numbers were being depleted through losses. Tired but determined, the cavalrymen and infantry held the defences over 22 and 23 October with rifles and a limited number of machine guns. The Germans then began to feel that the British positions were too strong and the rifle and machine gun too accurate, and so they decided they were not able to take Messines until able to launch a fresh attack with heavy artillery.

After spending a week trying other parts of the British line the Germans made a concerted effort to press the British again. A number of heavy guns had been placed and came into action on 30 October, pounding the defences and hoping to annihilate the British cavalry and infantry who had dug in. These troops, though, were thinly scattered and the heavy barrage caused few casualties; during the late morning the attackers opposite Hollebeke – the 3rd and 4th Bavarian Divisions – concentrated their heavy artillery on trenches around the village and chateau, causing the Royals of the Cavalry Brigade to vacate their positions, although this was carried out in a methodical manner, with the wounded being taken to safety. The 57th Wilde's Rifles near Oosttaverne came under heavy pressure and were surrounded, the 129th Baluchi Cavalry who went to their aid suffered over 200 losses. The Baluchis – Muslims from the Punjab, who were unused to the cold wet weather – had two machine guns which they used against the

The 129th Baluchis near Wytschaete at the end of October 1914. The trenches at this stage are shallow and rudimentary, as they are thought to be a temporary expedient. IWM. Q60744

Germans to great effect before the crews of Sepoys were killed. One of the Punjabis, Khudadad Khan, who was wounded, worked one of the machine guns alone for some time, and for his bravery under fire was later awarded the VC.

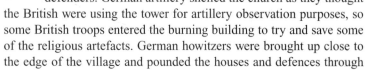

K. Khan, VC.

The hamlet of Wambeke had already fallen to the attackers. Messines village, where the Queen's Bays, Dragoon Guards and Hussars had made themselves ready with outer defences on the eastern side of the village, was attacked during the afternoon by Württembergers who were repulsed and unable to enter the village because of British rifle fire. A battery of British artillery, with 60 pounders, gave much assistance to the defenders. German artillery shelled the church as they thought the British were using the tower for artillery observation purposes, so some British troops entered the burning building to try and save some of the religious artefacts. German howitzers were brought up close to the edge of the village and pounded the houses and defences through

16

the night. Just before dawn on 31 October Germans of the 119 Grenadier and 125 Infantry Regiments, cheering, blowing horns and with some reportedly wearing turbans to confuse the defenders, made a sudden attack and captured some of the British line, which was not a continuous trench but a series of short lengths. Further attacks were made but the Germans were forced back; after a pause, during which time the heavy guns continued to bombard the defences, they tried again and this time met with some success. The British cavalry and the 2nd Inniskilling Fusiliers were forced back through the remains of the houses, many of which were on fire, to the western edge of the village. They did not want to be pushed back further as this would be down the steep slope on this side of the ridge. By noon the

German officers at a *Blinkstelle* or observation and signalling point near Messines watching the British through powerful binoculars. Their observations were used to direct the artillery.

front was along the main village street, the Wytschaete road (today the N365) and both the defenders and attackers were getting tired and desperate. The Germans brought up reinforcements to keep up the pressure and during the afternoon British aid also arrived. Troops of the 2nd King's Own Scottish Borderers and 2nd King's Own Yorkshire Light Infantry, professional, fully trained soldiers although inexperienced in combat, worked their way up the western slope and into the village to assist the defenders. To the north of the village, on the crest of the ridge, the London Scottish (14th London Regiment) also arrived on the scene as daylight was fading. These were Territorials, the first part time soldiers to enter the fighting, men with relatively little training who had up till now been carrying out duties well away from the fighting. Their mixed skills had been used as military police, guards and labourers, they had been receiving confusing orders and counter-orders and had been in Wytschaete ready

Detachment of London Scottish after their action at Messines.

to fight there when sent to Messines. The road along the ridge was unusable due to the fighting so, under Lieutenant Colonel Malcolm, the 750 kilted London Scottish made their way along the western slope, past L'Enfer Farm, to counter-attack on the northern edge of the village, near the windmill which stood there. They stormed up the slope, past 4 Huns Farm, which had been prepared for defence by the 1st Field Squadron, Royal Engineers under Captain Jordan, to engage the Germans, who saw them coming as they reached the crest and crossed the road. Artillery and machine gun fire rained upon the Territorials, those who got through this to reach the front line reinforced the cavalrymen and fought the German 122nd Fusiliers. Both sides fought hard, with the battle going on into the night. The London Scottish had problems with their rifles which kept jamming because of incompatible bullets and by the end of the action the London Scottish had lost 321 out of 750 men.

The fighting for Messines village had been severe and cost many casualties, however as the Germans had been successful to the north it was decided to evacuate the ruins and for the garrison to retire to the lower ridge at Wulvergem at 9am on 1 November. The village of

18

EARL HAIG

KING ALBERT

Above: Is the ceremony of the dedication of the memorial by King Albert of Belgium (wearing cap) in May 1923. He is accompanied by Douglas (by then Earl) Haig.

Left: The memorial to the 1st Battalion London Scottish by the N365 on the crest of of Messines Ridge. The St. Andrew's cross is on the site of the windmill which stood here.

Wytschaete had meanwhile been lost to the British. The Bavarians had made several attempts to take it; attack after attack left many dead on both sides and eventually they broke in and took control. The 1st Northumberland Fusiliers and 1st Lincolnshires, with the assistance of some of the 32nd French Division, counter- attacked in a bid to take Wytschaete back, but the Bavarians were ready for them and progress was not possible. The Northumberlands and Lincolnshires dug in on the edge of the village under heavy artillery and machine gun fire from within the village and Wytschaete Wood, they took high casualties before retiring to high ground at Spanbroekmolen.

Whilst the British and Germans kept up the fight further to the north opposite Ypres, between Wytschaete and Messines the lines were now more or less settled, and were to stay in much the same place for some time. The Germans now had the high ground of Messines Ridge, and the Steenbeek valley to the west with Wytschaete while the British,

German infantry reinforcements (ablösung) in a village behind the lines, ready to relieve another unit in the front line (Schützengraben).

with the French on their left, still held the high ground of Hill 63 which overlooked and protected the British front and the Douve valley. The Germans enjoyed good observation over the British lines in front of Messines Ridge, which enabled accurate artillery bombardments. During one heavy bombardment by German batteries situated behind Messines on the British lines held by the 1st Duke of Cornwall's Own Infantry on 20 November Bandsman Thomas Rendle, operating as stretcher bearer, won the VC for rescuing men buried by the shelling, dragging himself and wounded through the mud under artillery and sniper fire.

The British had a last attempt to recapture Wytschaete; on 14 December, after No. 1 Siege Battery of the Royal Garrison Artillery had pounded the German lines with 6" howitzer shells, the 1st Gordon Highlanders and the 2nd Royal Scots, of the 3rd Division, took over the British front line opposite Petit Bois in preparation and made an attack at 7.45 am, but the Bavarian defenders also were ready. The Scotsmen had to cross about 250 metres of open ground, which was swept by machine gun fire and field artillery before they met the German barbed wire: the Gordons had difficulty crossing this but the Royal Scots were luckier, they reached the German lines and took forty two Bavarian prisoners before being forced to retire back to the British lines. One of the Royal Scots, Private Henry

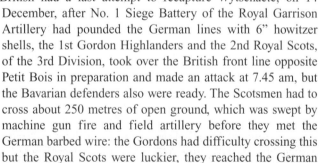

T. Rendle, VC.

Robson, distinguished himself by rescuing wounded men under fire, being wounded himself in the act. He was later awarded the VC. The attack was resumed on 15 and 16 December, but the British made no gains and the attack fizzled out.

H. Robson, VC.

Both sides had realised that they they were to be here for some time, and tried to make themselves as comfortable as possible in the circumstances. The cold, wet Flemish weather set in for the winter; trenches became filled with mud and water, sandbag barricades collapsed, and any new excavations were spotted by the ever watchful foe 200 metres away who brought down artillery fire on the work and the workers. The 1st Northumberland Fusiliers, in trenches opposite Petit Bois, were issued on 25 November with thick fur waistcoats. Their commander could not decide if this should be worn over the greatcoat, which made the wearer very conspicuous, or under it, which in most cases made the coat so tight that it interfered with the men's movement when firing.

The Northumberlands also received other goods and stores, not much of which was found to be perfectly suited to the conditions. Braziers were found to be good but the coke provided was quite difficult to start without causing large flames and smoke, which attracted the Germans' attention, and periscopes were useful but as they were made of cardboard these were unserviceable. A Very Pistol, to fire flares, was received but the Northumberlands did not like the

Wytschaete today from the site of the British front line, showing the ground over which the Royal Scots and the Gordons attacked. The bushes in the foreground are approximately on the site of the German front line. The road on the left was named Suicide Road. On the left of the road and up towards Wytschaete was also the ground over which the Irishmen attacked the village, on top of the long slope, on the morning of 7 June 1917. On the right of the road was the Ulster's area, Just behind the bushes was the strongpoint of Peckham, under which a mine was exploded.

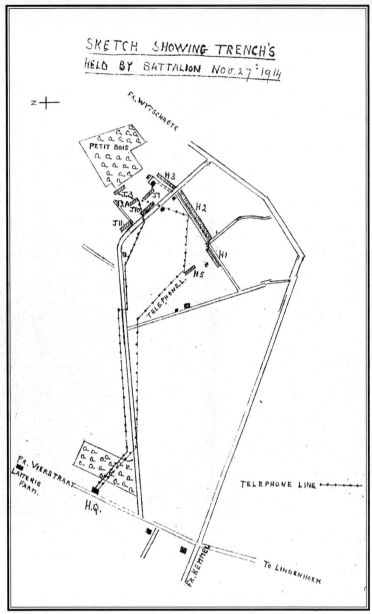

Map of the front held by the 1st Northumberland Fusiliers, in trenches in front of Petit Bois which was occupied by the Germans. This battalion was one of the first units to have telephone links between the front line trenches and the Battalion Headquarters dugout. The equipment was not official issue but privately donated to the Battalion in late November. The front line trenches, at this stage not fully connected or continuous, were given reference numbers as the system of grid line map references was not yet in being (see map of the lettered zones, p.33). The front line trenches were to remain in the same positions through 1915, 1916 and the first half of 1917, over which period trench names were adopted and communication and support trenches added.

German working party building up the defences around Messines in the winter of 1914. Several have obviously already been involved in the fighting as they are wearing the ribbon of the Iron Cross on the second button.

projectile, considering that a slower burning light would increase effectiveness. Experiments with a new device, Hale's Rifle Grenade, were not successful as detonation was found to need a high angle of fire, with the rifle held high.

Christmas Day 1914 found the Territorials of the 6th Cheshires, men from Stockport and surrounding villages, in the front trenches opposite Messines. They had spent the last few nights stood in the frozen mud of the trenches just in front of Stinking Farm (some cattle had been killed there during the early fighting and were now bloated corpses) and some men suffered from frost bite. The artillery fired a few rounds at the Germans at dawn and the men stood-to as normal. During the course of the morning Germans were seen clambering out of their trenches so the Cheshires fired rifle shots at them. The Germans, who were found to be Saxons of the 134th Infantry Regiment, waved Christmas Trees at the Cheshires who, at first suspicious, slowly rose from their own trench and strolled into No Man's Land. A football was found and kicked around and souvenirs of buttons and badges exchanged, and some of the dead who had been lying around were buried, but during the afternoon men were ordered back to their trenches and the truce was over.

Time spent in the trenches through the first winter – 1914/15– were similar for troops on both sides of No Man's Land. Trenches were dug and repaired, sandbags filled and placed to increase the effective depth, hollows and dugouts scraped out of the trench walls for shelter, and wiring parties crept out each night to form barbed wire entanglements, supported on wooden and iron supports, as quietly as possible. Patrols went out on most nights to try and prevent enemy use of the ground between the front lines, and to gain information on the other side's activities. Many periods of shell fire, much of it very heavy, had to be endured, as did the sudden raking of trenches with machine gun fire and the ever present threat of sniper fire for the unwary.

Adolf Hitler, the Little Corporal at Wytschaete and Messines.

On 1 August 1914 Germany declared war on Russia, and two days later on France. A struggling young artist living in Munich was delighted at the news, and immediately petitioned, as an Austrian, the King of Bavaria to join the Bavarian Army. He was accepted and enlisted into the 16th Bavarian Reserve Infantry Regiment, known as the List Regiment after its first commanding officer, Colonel von List, and was to spend time on Messines Ridge.

Adolf Hitler had been trying to make a living as an artist in Munich, without any great success, since 1912. After failing to sell paintings in Vienna he had left Austria in disgust; he considered that the Hapsburg Empire was a degenerate drain on German policy, on the point of disintegration and morally corrupt. The suicide in May 1913 of an important military polititian, Colonel Alfred Rendl, a homosexual who had been blackmailed into giving military secrets to Russia, deepened his dislike of the Austrian Army. Whilst he was in Munich the Austrian Army traced him to No. 34 Schleissheimerstrasse and, through the

Adolf Hitler (seated, with moustache) during his time with the 16th Bavarian Reserve Infantry Regiment. From the second button on his tunic he wears the ribbon of the Iron Cross.

German local officials, summonsed him and tried to conscript him into the army. Hitler made a plea for clemency, claiming that he was not fit enough for military service and physically weak. His protestations worked and he was exempted from military duty and declared 'unfit for combat and auxiliary duties, too weak, and unable to bear arms.'

He was therefore allowed to continue his bohemian existence, during which time he developed some skills of oratory although he made little impact on those who heard his tirades about Marxists and Jews. He was considered to be a loner and a crank. Living in a boarding house he made no friends and few aquaintances except his landlord, a tailor named Herr Popp.

When war came he was delighted to be allowed to join, as a foreigner, the German Army; soon he was marching to the training and exercise camp at Lechfeld with the other new and enthusiastic volunteers. Also recruited into the 16th Bavarian R.I.R. was a volunteer Hitler was to know well in later years, Rudolf Hess.

The 16th Bavarian R.I.R. was soon sent to the front, in late October 1914 they were entrained for Lille, now in German hands, and marched

Left: **German soldiers outside a dugout near the ruins of Messines Church. Hitler served in this trench system as a regimental runner from 1914 until the summer of 1916 and regularly took shelter in the church crypt. The church was badly damaged in 1914; it suffered more damage from shells in 1915 (at which stage Corporal Hitler painted it) and 1916, and was in complete ruins, (as shown in the photograph above) after the 1917 fighting. The crypt, used as a German shelter, is today a shrine to Countess Adela, who died here in 1079 AD.**

Right: **The church of St. Nicholas, Messines, today. The church is a prominent landmark visible from all around the ridge and is a good aid to navigation. The style is based on the Abbey church which was not re-built.**

up through Wervick towards Ypres. Hitler's regiment took enormous losses (349 killed on the first day) during the fighting with the British during the last days of October at Beselare and Gheluvelt, near Ypres, the high losses being attributed to appalling and incompetent leadership; Colonel von List himself was killed on 29 October.

The first days of November saw the Bavarians and Hitler, now gaining an impression that he had somehow been saved by Providence, trying to press the British further back off Messines Ridge and through Wytschaete and the Wood. The fighting was bitter with many losses on both sides and Hitler was generally in the thick of it, apparently showing much bravery on several occasions. Hitler was promoted to corporal and wrote home to his landlord, Herr Popp (not having anyone else to write to) describing how many men had been lost;

> 'But we were all proud of having licked the Britishers. Since then we have been in the front lines the whole time. I was proposed for the Iron Cross, the first time in Messines, the second time in Wytschaete. On 2 December I finally got it'

He had been awarded the Iron Cross, 2nd Class. This also changed his outlook on his own status: he and three others were asked to step out of the officer's small, cramped dug-out near Wytschaete while this was discussed and as he went outside a British shell landed on the roof; all inside were killed or wounded, including the commanding officer, Lieutenant-Colonel Engelhardt. Long after the war, in 1932, Engelhardt testified for Hitler in a lawsuit against a Hamburg paper which had accused Hitler of cowardice:

> 'As commander of the 16th Regiment of Bavarian Infantry I came to know Adolf Hitler as an exceedingly brave, effective and conscientious soldier. I must emphasise the following; as our men were storming the wood [Petit Bois] I stepped out of the woods near Wytschaete to get a better view of developments. Hitler and the other volunteer, Bachmann, stood before me to protect me with their bodies from the machine gun fire to which I was exposed'

Soon after Hitler and the Bavarians clashed with the British at Wytschaete the lines stabilised, leaving the Bavarians in this village and Messines. Apart from being promoted to corporal Hitler was given the job of Meldeganger or despatch runner, with the task of carrying messages between company and Regimental headquarters, front lines and rear stations. This was a dangerous post which apparently Hitler carrried out well, having several narrow escapes from imminent death, each occurence reinforcing his belief in divine providence and his idea that he had been chosed to survive.

During his quiet periods at the front Hitler spent his free time reading political books and painting scenes around Messines Ridge. He made no friends in his Regiment, his colleagues disliked his rantings when excited, his only close friend was his dog, Fuchsl (Foxy).

In late January Hitler wrote again to his landlord in Munich, Herr Popp, describing the area:

'For the past two months our regiment has been constanly in the front line between Messines and Wytschaete. The meadows and the fields look like bottomless swamps, while the roads are covered ankle deep in mud. Through these swamps run the trenches of our infantry, a maze of dug- outs and trenches with loopholes. The air has been trembling under the screams and the roar of grenades and the bursting of shells. What is most dreadful is when the guns begin to spit across the whole front at night....but nothing is ever going to shift us from here.'

He painted several scenes around Messines and its ruined church, beneath which was the crypt in which was a command centre he carried messages from, and Wytschaete, a number of which still survive and occasionally turn up at art auctions, fetching prices of £3,000-5,000 in the 1990's, not for any artistic merit but for the signature attached. A copy of a Hitler painting of Messines church, said to be one he favoured and kept in his office when in power in Berlin, hangs in Messines museum.

Hitler spent the rest of the war years as a messenger and was not promoted higher than corporal, despite being a brave soldier, and in a time, especially later in the war, when the ranks were trawled for experienced men and potential officers were in short supply. He was considered to be not able to lead men and probably was mentally unstable. Hitler also saw action at Neuve-Chapelle, La Bassée, and the Somme, where he was wounded in the left thigh on 5th October 1916 near Warlencourt, Bapaume (if only that bullet had been a little higher....). After treatment and convalescence back in Germany he returned to the front in time for fighting at Arras and Ypres in 1917. In August 1918 he was awarded the Iron Cross, 1st Class, 'for personal cold-blooded bravery and continuous readiness to sacrifice himself' near Reims. This decoration was given to him by his commanding officer, Hugo Gutmann, a Jew, which later caused Hitler and his image makers some embarrassment. Hitler was again in Flanders; on the night of 13 October 1918, as the British were pushing the Germans back at La Montagne, near Wervick, he was gassed and invalided back to Pasewalk, near Berlin, and then Munich, where he stayed and caused political turmoil after the war ended.

One of Hitler's early political opponents was Hans Mend, who had been Hitler's immediate superior in the Bavarian Army. Mend published in 1931 a pamphlet titled *'Adolf Hitler in the Field, 1914-1916'*, relating Hitler's part in the war, and in a later publication, 1933,

named the Mend Report, wrote that when Hitler was in the trenches he
*'made long muddled speeches to the men...and made little
clay figures, stood them in a row on the parapet and harangued
them about how, after the war was won, social order would be
changed and a new order set up. More and more his comrades
came to look on him as an absurd braggart and a crazy
chatterbox whom no one could take seriously.'*
Soon after this Report came out Mend disappeared from the streets of
Munich after being asked to attend a meeting with the newly formed
Gestapo; he was never seen again.

Hitler returned to Messines Ridge at least twice in the early 1940s
when Germany occupied Belgium; he visited Croonart Wood where he
had spent some time (the wood was until recent years preserved by the
owner as a trench museum) and Bethlehem Farm near Messines, where
he had been billeted for a time; on this visit he presented the farmer's
wife with a bunch of flowers.

Chapter Two

1915. TRENCH STALEMATE

The opening months of 1915 were not kind to the soldiers in the front line trenches. The New Year had ushered in snow and freezing, icy winds, with cold rain resulting in trenches and dugouts being flooded and collapsing; Royal Engineers worked on schemes to dam and drain trenches which were soon to be filled with water again, the heavy clay of the region making natural drainage very slow. Tools and equipment required to improve drainage – shovels and picks, sandbags and wood for duckboards and revetting – had not been held in great numbers by the Army as this type of static warfare had not been experienced before. The situation was worse for those Regular soldiers who had recently been shipped in to Belgium and France from parts of the Empire, such as India, Aden and Suez, who had not been through a European winter for some years, their blood thin from hot climates. Some troops standing knee deep in frozen mud and slush needed to be relieved twice daily, and the sickness rate, largely from frozen feet and circulatory problems, ('trench foot') soared; for men living outside, with limited food and shelter, German bullets were not the only problem. Lines were manned by thinner numbers as manpower became an increasing problem.

Constant shelling by the Germans was not matched by the British, as artillery was in short supply, and the small numbers of field guns

Trenches near Wytschaete.

Right: Infantry commander's map of the British trenches in front of Wytschaete, early 1915, written on an older Belgian land map. The front line is not yet continuous but is still a series of disjointed sections, although the German front line is shown as complete (compare with Northumberland Fusiliers earlier map of trenches in zones H and J, page 22). The British front is divided into lettered zones, and each trench within each zone is numbered, e.g. J3 and G4, for administrative and navigational purposes. Some had by now been given names by troops but these were not yet officially adopted. As both sides dug in for siege warfare the trench systems became more and more complicated, with support, rear and communications trenches. During 1915 the British re-mapped the whole of the front, often in dangerous circumstances, and the squared grid system of co-ordinates which enabled any location to be accurately given. The British names for the German trenches related to the map square which covered them: those in square N were named Naples Trench, Nail Trench, Narrow Trench and many others beginning with N; those in Square O were named Object Trench, Oblige Trench and others beginning with O, and those in square U all began with U - Uhlan Trench, Ulcer Trench etc.

and howitzers were desperately short of ammunition, shells being rationed to four per gun per day. Territorial troops began to arrive as reinforcements to the Regulars, and had to learn the ways of the new warfare. The 1st Cambridgeshires arrived in the sector opposite St, Eloi early in March, and were given work on the support lines whilst being introduced to life in the the front lines. The Royal Engineer officer in charge of the trench digging was surprised at how quickly the Cambridgeshires completed their first task, not realising the men were largely from the Fens, with hereditary skills in digging drains and dykes. Each company spent time in the firing line; Corporal Jones wrote home relating his first experience of being in the firing line which ran through St. Eloi village and having his first taste of fire:

> *'A greater scene of desolation would be hard to realise. There seemed no building but had been shattered, and everywhere was deserted, save for a few cats and a few of the animals which had escaped the fusilade. One was set thinking by the continuous whine of the bullets and shells singing quite close to us, and by the 'phut' of the bullet as it found its resting place in a wall or roof.'*

The Cambridgeshires were soon to be involved in a full scale battle, as the Germans repeated earlier attempts to capture St. Eloi and The Mound, a heap of spoil from an old brickworks nearby, about ten metres high and 100 metres across. This had given the British a good

WYTSCHAETE.

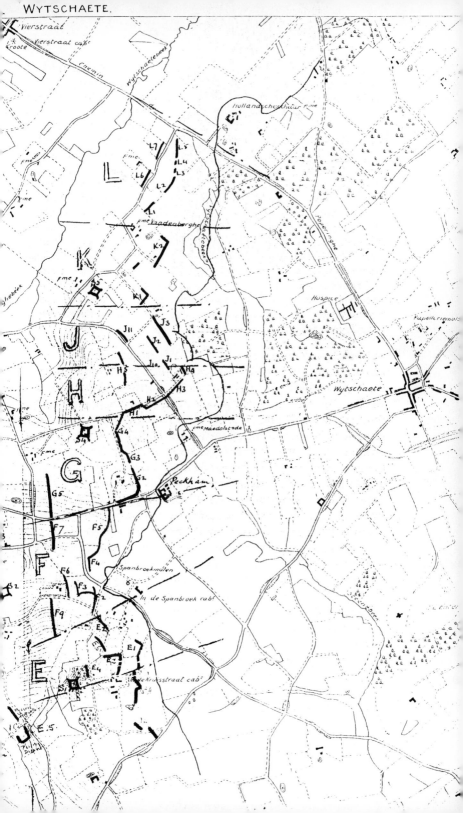

Members of the Honourable Artillery Company clean their rifles in a front line trench at St. Eloi, 1915.

vantage point, two machine guns were sited there, and the Germans wanted to take control of it. They had tried several times in February, and at 5.30pm on 14 March they launched a surprise major attack, beginning with a method which was to become a frequent occurence here. The German miners had been busy for some time, and the two mines they fired under the British front line were successful in eliminating the machine guns on The Mound and causing disorganisation among the defenders. Storming the smoking mine craters the Germans, led by assault troops carrying only light arms and hand grenades, pushed back the 2nd King's Shropshire Light Infantry and the 4th Rifle Brigade beyond the front trenches and through St. Eloi. Battalions on either side of the immediate front attacked were forced to retire as the German advance made them vulnerable to fire from the side, in enfilade. By the time it was dark the Germans were in full possession of St. Eloi and their engineers moved in quickly to organise the village ruins for defence. Machine gun posts and protection from gun fire were established, with barbed wire barricades across the streets.

The British, with the assistance of the the Irishmen of the 1st Royal Irish, 2nd Royal Irish Fusiliers and the 1st Leinsters began a counter-attack at two in the morning. Fighting their way through the defences they took back the ruins of the village and trenches, the German defenders were tenacious but the attackers were determined. The Germans were pushed back to the edge of the village, a small party of Royal Irish under Second Lieutenant Ford and Sergeant Brown rushed the German position at the last house in the village but all were killed or wounded. The counter-attack had been largely successful but the Germans remained in control of the The Mound despite the pressure applied by the Royal Irish. The Germans considered the operation a success as they now had the high ground they wanted; the attack had been an isolated action with limited objectives.

When the fighting was over the streets of St. Eloi were littered with dead and dying British and Germans. Two Irishmen, Company Sergeant Major Kelsey and Lance Corporal Carrol, began to collect the wounded under the gaze of the Germans, including wounded men from off the wire immediately in front of the German line. A German officer signalled them to go away, which they did with the last of the wounded. Similar acts of mutual humanity were to become much more rare.

Whilst to the north the Battles of Ypres raged on and saw changes in warfare with the use of gas, and to the south fighting was to be heavy at Aubers, Festubert and Loos the fighting in and around St. Eloi

British support trench running through the ruins of St. Eloi in the spring of 1915. As the situation above ground became more dangerous the house cellars were connected to the growing trench system. IWM Q52004

was the last organised battle in 1915 on this sector, and the troops in the front lines and supports in front of Messines-Wytschaete-St. Eloi settled down to the monotony and routine of trench life. Although the sector was a 'quiet' sector the artillery, snipers and trench raiders took a daily toll on the troops. The British launched small scale assaults to

C. Martin, VC.

prevent the Germans opposite from being transferred to reinforce other sectors where the British were attacking. A typical operation on 12 March was where the Germans held the hill at Spanbroekmolen, and the British wanted them to remain there rather than join the fighting going on Neuve Chapelle. The attack on the hill began in the early afternoon but Germans in one stretch of trench held up the advance. A Royal Engineer officer, Lieutenant Cyril Martin, led a group of six men armed with early versions of hand grenades. Although hampered by a bullet wound he bombed the Germans out of the trench and organised the small party to turn the trench round, changing the parapet to consolidate it for defence and

Hiele Form.
O·8·d·95·95

Dome House.
O·8·d·9¾·6¾

View from 1·31·c·5½·2

O·9·b·0·5½

View from O·1·a 6¾·3½

In den Jager Cab.ᵗ
O·8·d·9¾·2¼

Sketch of the ruins of Dome House and other buildings at the top end of the Dammstrasse, made by a British intelligence officer at a vantage point behind the lines in Voormezele, about 1½ kilometers distant. At this stage the British were interested in finding out the purpose of some posts where construction work was apparent, these later turned out to be concrete machine gun emplacements

View from 1·31·a·5½·2

held it for several hours until ordered to retire as the assault ended. For his action Martin was awarded the VC. A month later, on 12 April, the 1st Royal Irish Fusiliers were holding the line where it crossed the Douve River opposite Petite Douve Farm when the Germans began a particularly heavy artillery bombardment. Many Irishmen were killed by the shells, and several were buried by the explosions; Private Robert

R. Morrow, VC.

Morrow distinguished himself by digging out some buried and wounded men and, while shells fell around him, several times he crossed the river to reach trapped men. He was awarded the VC for his bravery under fire.

Canada had been represented at the front since Princess Patricia's Canadian Light Infantry (named after the daughter of the Duke of Connaught, the Governor-General, and nicknamed 'Pat's Pets') had taken over the front line at St. Eloi earlier in the year. The 1st and 2nd Canadian Divisions took over the front and organised themselves and their defences to prevent any German forays from the heights of the Ridge. The Germans dominated the field with observation from the high ground but the Canadians came to the fore when darkness fell. Trench raids of varying sizes were mounted and the Canadians made a point of patrolling and controlling No Man's Land at night. The Canadians

also kept a watchful eye on the Germans in the villages and the slopes of the Ridge, with telescopes and periscopes, reporting each detail observed during the day – work on trenches and emplacements, new wire and stakes and all troop and personnel movements. German officers were seen to visit positions. All information was compiled into Intelligence Reports; a typical day's report for the middle of September gives

The Germans were the first to strengthen their machine gun posts with concrete. This sketch, from 1915, shows an early example of protection for the gunner.

The troops on both sides of No Man's Land had long periods when little happened. These German officers are playing cards only a few hundred metres from the British.

information on an opening in the road barricade on the Messines-Stinking Farm road, two working parties near Petite Douve Farm and alterations to two machine gun posts near by.

Although the Messines sector was a relatively quiet one during 1915 and into 1916, troops were kept busy while in the front line and 'at rest'. Trenches were being continually repaired, artillery gun pits dug, shell proof cover improved and roads levelled. As the summer and autumn gave way to winter some attention was also given to troop

MESSAGES AND SIGNALS.

Prefix .... Code .... m.	Words	Charge	*This message is on a/o of:*	Recd. at .... m
Office of Origin and Service Instructions.				Date ....
....	Sent		.... *Service.*	From ....
....	At .... m.			
....	To			By ....
....	By	(Signature of " Franking Officer.")		

TO   4th Canadian Inf Bde

Sender's Number. ＊ A 12	Day of Month. 28	In reply to Number.	A A A

Artillery - Enemy sent 19 whiz-bangs over about 100
yds in rear of our front trenches at 3 pm No damage
evidently they were after our working parties. Machine
Gun and rifle fire were light both day and night Last
evening about 6 bombs mostly rifle grenades came over-
One landed in our trenches wounding 5 men. Aeroplanes
and Balloons - nil. Our snipers report one periscope
and also report one German shot while walking along
exposing himself above parapet.
Some bombers were seen being carried in German trenches
in front of M 1 Bay 19 Enemy are generally quiet
Our work - Building dugouts draining, improving parapets, laying trench gratings and 175 men under Engineers

From   ADJT   19th Bn

Place

Time   6 10 pm

The above may be forwarded as now corrected.

.... Censor.   **(Z)**   Thos Morrison Capt Adjt

Signature of Addressor or Person authorised to telegraph in his name.

* This line should be erased if not required.

225,000. W 14042—M 44. H. W. & V., Ld. 12/15.

A typical daily report, for 15 October 1915, from the 19th Canadian
Infantry Battalion, a front line battalion facing Messines Ridge, to
Brigade Headquarters. A fairly quiet day, with working parties of both
sides under threat and the target for the other side's artillery and snipers.
In the busier periods during battles and operations, battalions did not
have the ordered luxury of typed reports although daily battalion diaries
were always kept up to date, usually hand written.

accommodation and equipment but the men were again having to endure cold and wet conditions and had little means of sheltering from the elements. The Flanders rain was heavy and trenches filled with water or collapsed despite the drainage systems, sandbag breastworks dissolved, and dugouts flooded. Rubber waders were issued to front line troops, together with supplies of clean socks and oil to waterproof boots. Trench Foot, which had been prevalent in the 1914/15 winter, was made into a punishable offence although the ailment was still common and affected many hundreds of men. Exposure to the weather also resulted in respiratory and other diseases. The Germans on the higher ground of the Ridge also suffered from cold but they were able to arrange drainage of their trenches, often into the lower lying Canadian trenches where possible.

Christmas 1915 arrived, and both sides refrained from firing. Any fraternisation with the Germans, as had happened the previous Christmas, had been specifically banned by British High Command but the Canadian officers were less strict, troops of both sides were able to walk about in the open in safety. No large scale fraternisation occurred but there was some communication and exchange of greetings between the two front lines.

Although the soldiers above ground had had a reasonably quiet time for much of 1915, below the surface the miners on both sides had been very busy. Each still wanted The Mound on the edge of St. Eloi and employed siege warfare tactics to try and gain control of the mud patch which existed there now. The German miners were driving mines up to ten metres deep and tunnelling beneath the British lines and the British had likewise been similarly active. The nerve-racking work was anything but easy, apart from the constant risks of gas and roof collapse as they worked through the sandy clay with some water-bearing sand, there was the constant threat of the opposition exploding camouflets, small mine charges designed to cause collapse. The blowing of mines was usually timed to coincide with infantry attacks, and the race was on to reach and consolidate the crater lips before the enemy did. The attackers hoped that the front line defenders had been obliterated but often an assault had been expected and the front line was very lightly garrisoned, with troops in support trenches ready to race forward and drive off the attackers. By the end of 1915 a total of 33 mines and 31 camouflets had been blown by both sides around The Mound, which was by now greatly reduced in height, but the front lines had hardly moved. In August, to offset the stalemate caused by the two sides mining at similar levels, the British began a scheme of deep

Germans behind the railway embankment at Hollebeke, above, and the same site today, with a replaced bridge, below. This provided an excellent shell proof wall for them between 1914 and 1918 and numerous dugouts and concrete shelters were constructed on the eastern side. It was later fortified with machine gun posts.

mining, sinking three shafts ot 20 metres deep, into the clay beneath the sand. The deep mining was carried out in great secrecy, with the spoil being concealed and taken away from the site in sandbags. Six tunnels were driven from the shafts, timed to be under the 500 metre stretch of the German front line opposite St. Eloi by early March 1916 for a large scale offensive: the British wanted to take control of The Mound and eliminate the German salient which it formed.

Chapter Three

1916. MINING AT THE MOUND

The Canadians saw in the New Year of 1916 in the trenches opposite Messines Ridge; the Canadian Corps was responsible for the front line stretching from south of the River Douve to St Eloi. The troops in the water-filled trenches were relieved after six days, and then spent six days at rest in reserve, then six days in the support trenches and then back to the front for another six days. The Canadians made a point of keeping up the pressure on the Germans, with a policy of wearing them down with regular aggressive trench raids, much sniping, and frequent artillery bombardments. The first raid soon followed the New Year; on the night of 2 January 65 men of the 25th Battalion raided the German front line in front of Wytschaete. The German wire was cut by hand by an advance group, but this gave the Germans some warning and the raiders had to retire without reaching their objective, the front line trench. A larger scale raid on the trenches at Spanbroekmolen was planned for the early morning of 31 January; troops of the 28th and 29th Battalions, with cork blackened faces, many of whom had been given special training in the use of hand grenades, crept across No Man's Land at 2.40am and fought their way into and along the German trenches. The objective of the raid was to lower German morale and security, destroy dugouts and take prisoners for identification and intelligence. A number of Germans were killed by the raiders, and several prisoners taken although most of these were killed whilst being taken back to the Canadian lines by German machine gunners. The raid had cost only two Canadian lives and was considered a huge success, others were to follow.

The Canadians had also been keeping themselves up to date on the Germans in front of and on Messines Ridge. Daily intelligence reports were made on all movements behind the enemy lines: any alterations to trench works or emplacements and any earth spoil or wire, working parties or any men seen. Officers were occasionally seen doing their rounds, sometimes in apparent ease, for example in one day's report, for 9 February, the 1st Canadian Battalion opposite Messines reported

'2 high ranking German officers, identifiable by braid and badges, observed in gateway at Birthday Farm'.

Other German officers also walked around as if in a safe area:

'23 February. A man wearing a light coloured raincoat,

without equipment, carried a big stick, accompanied by a big dog, came down path near Middle Farm'.

Life further along the line was not always so cushy, as Princess Patricia's Canadian Light Infantry, in front of the German stronghold of Peckham on 19 February recorded,

'Sniping very active, our men cannot reach the enemy at this point, and their front, which is very strong, needs smashing up with big guns'.

While the Canadians had been busy harassing and aggressively opposing the Germans, the British miners of 172 Tunnelling Company, Royal Engineers, had been continuing with their deep mines and tunnels at St Eloi. The Germans were still enjoying possession of The Mound, which, although by now significantly reduced in height following the numerous mines blows and heavy artillery bombardments, gave excellent observation over the British. The Mound was also the

Whilst the Canadians were watching the Germans, they were being watched themselves. This postcard sent home to Germany illustrates, 'Part of our support trench with observation post.'

central part of a German salient which jutted out into the British lines, at a slightly higher level than the surrounding terrain.

The troops of the 3rd Division practised for the forthcoming attack over a course at Reninghelst which simulated the terrain to be expected. Between 20 and 25 March they drilled and rehearsed all movements and positions. At 7pm on 26 March the first wave troops were conveyed by motor bus to Voormezeele, from where they marched through St Eloi to the assembly trenches, the 1st Battalion Northumberland Fusiliers on the west of the village, and the 4th Royal Fusiliers on the east (the trenches in front of St Eloi here ran from east to west). The plan was for these two battalions to start the attack

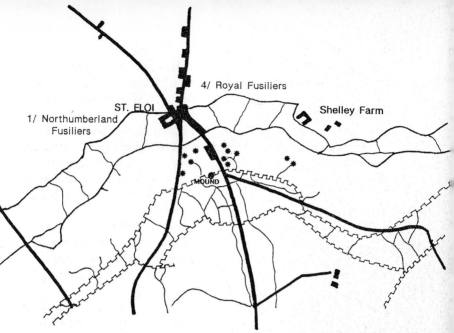

The British and German lines at St. Eloi just before the attack by the 1st Northumberland Fusiliers and 4th Royal Fusiliers on 27 March 1916. The German front line includes The Mound, which gave good observation over the British. The area of No Man's Land contained many smaller craters from earlier mine warfare, at this time most of them were nominally held by the Germans as listening posts and forward positions. Deep underground six mines were being prepared for blowing beneath the German front line as a prelude to the attack, four large (2,3,4 and 5, with no. 3 directly under The Mound) and 1 and 6 on the flank to provide cover. The first objective was to be the resultant craters, the attackers were then to take the main objective, the German second line, cutting off the salient and occupying the high ground.

immediately following the detonation of the six mines, but as the resultant craters would form serious obstacles and be heavily shelled by the Germans, the two battalions would occupy the German support lines then work their way to meet behind the craters, having cut off the salient. Other battalions would then come up as reinforcements to consolidate the gains and repel the expected counter-attack.

The 18th Reserve Jäger Battalion holding the The Mound and the German trenches considered an attack to be likely at some time, but were not aware of the presence of the six mines, which were much deeper than theirs and had not been suspected. The positions of the mines had been carefully thought out by the British planners: mines 1 and 6 were relatively small, on the flank of the attack, whilst number 3

See map
p.46

was the largest of the lot and was designed to remove The Mound and leave a large crater. Mines 2, 4 and 5 were to remove strongpoints in the trench system.

As the attack was to be a surprise, a preliminary artillery bombardment was not used to cut the German wire as the mine explosions would remove this. The initial salvo was also timed so that the various heavy guns and howitzers used, the shells of which had differing trajectories and flight times, would reach their objectives simultaneousely.

The night of 26/27 March was very cold with snow and sleet; the Northumberlands and Royal Fusiliers who were huddled in their starting positions, were not wearing greatcoats and had a rough time waiting. At 4.15am the gloomy light was rent apart as, with a roar, the mines exploded with giant flames leaping into the air. The eruptions, whilst obliterating the featureson the surface and leaving gaping craters, caused trenches on both sides to collapse. It had been calculated that the débris from the mines would take 30 seconds to fall so the infantry were timed to begin their attack at 4.15am. The Northumberlands saw the last clods and earth falling before the 30 seconds were up and so decided not to wait. With ladders they scaled their parapets and went towards the German lines. They found the German wire, which was strong barbed concertina and plain concertina mixed, had not been destroyed, but the impetous could not be stopped and the men worked their way through the wire and into the German trenches. The decision not to wait the 30 seconds after the mine proved to be fortuitous, as a red flare went up from the German support line and a heavy German artillery barrage then fell onto the front trenches just vacated by the Northumberlands. Little resistance was met as the German infantry in the trenches were either buried by the mines or dazed and confused by the force of the explosions. One machine gun in the German front trench near where it crossed the

The Ist Northumberland Fusiliers, many with souvenirs, jubilant after their success on 27 March.

Messines road came into action, firing wildly into the dark at the attacking Northumberlands as they crossed the wire. Second Lieutenant H. J. Holmes and Lance Corporal M. Keirsey, who had got through the wire, rushed the machine gun and killed its crew of five; both were later awarded a medal (the Military Cross for the officer and the Distinguished Conduct Medal for the infantryman) for this action.

At 4.45 the Northumberlands had reached their objective, the German second line behind the salient, and began to send back their prisoners, whilst organising the newly won trenches against any German counter-attack. German snipers, watching the Northumberlands from their right and well to the rear, took a toll; at 8.15am the Germans launched a determined bid to push the British back. Parties with plentiful supplies of grenades worked their way along the trenches, trying to force the Northumberlands to surrender or retreat, causing many casualties to the new defenders, who had used most of their stock of grenades. The resultant bombing fight on the flank, during which the Northumberlands under Lieutenant C.B. Carrick held off the Germans using a stock of German grenades they had discovered, lasted

$2^1/_2$ hours; eventually the remnants of the German bombing party, two officers and 35 men, surrendered to Lieutenant Carrick and his force of four men. Lieutenant Carrick was awarded the Military Cross for holding off the Germans during this action.

Whilst the Northumberlands had been successful in reaching and holding their objectives, the 4th Royal Fusiliers on their left, near Shelley Farm, had been less fortunate. In the landscape which had been completely changed by the mine explosions the Fusiliers had made for the wrong craters and suffered many losses, including most of their officers, from machine gunners on their left. They reached craters in No Man's Land but were unable to get closer to the German front line. Support battalions, the 1st Royal Scots Fusiliers and the 12th West Yorkshires, with reinforcements and supplies, were to have reached the craters by communication trenches formed by explosions in pipes six feet below the surface which had been pushed forward from the British lines, but these had merely destroyed the existing trenches. The support battalions had therefore to dig new trenches across No Man's Land, which was difficult owing to the amount of wire in the ground and the persistent sniping and artillery shelling by the Germans. The shelling of the British went on throughout the day, with some periods being very heavy. Many of the trenches were filled with water and the troops made what shelter they could.

As darkness fell the British were holding their gains on the right but had made little ground on the left. The survivors of the two attacking battalions, the Northumberlands and the Royal Fusiliers, who were by now completely exhausted, were withdrawn having lost 445 men between them. They had taken just over 200 German prisoners and killed many more; it was later estimated from German records that about 300 Germans had been killed or buried by the mine explosions.

Relief battalions took over the sector during the night of 27/28 March, craters 1, 2, 3 and 6 being the front line. Crater 3, where The Mound had been, and the other three formed the new front line whilst the Germans held craters 4 and 5. The line of muddy trenches and crater rims of wet loose earth was held for three days as both sides tried to shell out the other.

During these three days the Chaplain of the 9th Brigade, the Reverend Ernest Noel Mellish, (he was the Curate of St. Paul's, Deptford) went out into the mire of mud and shellholes, under heavy machine gun and shell fire to rescue wounded men. For his bravery and concern for the wounded the Reverend Mellish was awarded the VC. On 30 March a party of the 1st Gordon Highlanders and the 12th West Yorkshires worked their way through the mud to find crater 4 unoccupied but crater 5 held by German machine gunners and infantry, whom they were unable to remove. The British resolved to capture crater 5, now the only element of the objective of 27 March not held. At 2am on 3 April, after a short but heavy bombardment, the 8th King's Own stormed the crater. The German defenders held out for some time but were exhausted and incapable of hard fighting and during the morning the force of five officers and 77 men, who had been cut off and without food for three days, surrendered.

Rev. E.N. Mellish, VC.

As all of the original objectives had now been taken and the German salient had been eliminated, the British consolidated the sector. The British battalions were withdrawn and replaced by the 6th Canadian Infantry Brigade on the morning of 4 April. The Canadians found the defences to be in a deplorable condition, with no continuous trenches, broken parapets and little barbed wire. Water filled shell holes formed much of the defences and the featureless area of mud gave no indication of the whereabouts of the German front line or positions. Dead and wounded British and Germans still lay around, many half buried in the mud. The Canadians tried to drain the shallow

The new British line, shown dotted, after the last parts of the objective for 27 March were captured on 3 April. The new line was handed over to the Canadians on 4 April; they consolidated the defences but were unable to resist the German attack of 6 April. The Germans had regained all the ground lost and the British were back in their original lines three hours after it started.

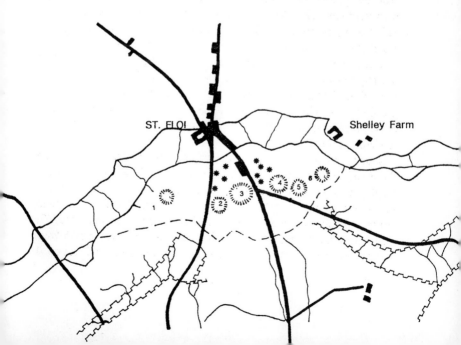

ST. ELOI   Shelley Farm

British pill box at St. Eloi. This was built late in 1917, on the western rim of the 7 June mine crater, sited to cover any German attack on the slight rise on which had sat The Mound before the 1916 mines. The corrugated iron formwork is apparent on the outside; the 'elephant iron' inner lining is still in good condition. No. 22 on map, page 135.

trenches, but found this difficult, and strengthened the defences as much as possible under the circumstances, expecting the Germans to attack and try to retake the area of the craters before long. They decided to hold the rear of the craters as being safer than the front, as the British battalions had done. The Canadians were subjected to continuous artillery bombardment whilst they re-organised their defences, during the night of 5/6 April the shelling was intensified and

Crater no. 4, blown on 27 March 1916, as it is today, a muddy, turbid pond used by local fishermen for relaxation. It was in the mud in and around this crater that the 4th Royal Fusiliers, 1st GordonHighlanders and others had some terrible problems, as did the Canadians who lost it to the Germans on 6 April. Crater no. 5, of similar size and condition, is still adjacent.

at 3.30am Germans of the 214th and 216th Reserve Regiments moved to take the craters. The Canadians were caught off balance as the front line battalion, the 27th, was in the process of being relieved by the 29th. The exchange was partially complete when the attackers struck,

centring on the road from Oosttaverne (the N336): isolated pockets of Canadians put up strong resistance but most were overwhelmed and not seen again. Reinforcing parties repeated the mistakes made by the Royal Fusiliers, confusing craters 4 and 5, which they claimed to control, with other, smaller ones, when the Germans were swarming over and and setting up machine gun positions there. After three hours of infiltration the Germans had recaptured all of the ground lost on 27 March, the front lines of both sides were back where they had been before the battle. Artillery of both sides carried out

This crater at St Eloi has been successfully captured by the Germans and turned into a strongpoint in their defence line. Within the relative safety of the hole, the soldiers are free to walk about without fear of being sniped.

heavy shelling of front and rear positions for the next two weeks and the area of mud and desolation spread outwards. The British then scaled down their artillery bombardments as they started to save ammunition for the attack being planned down on the Somme.

Soldiers of both sides were glad to see an end to the fighting around the muddy craters at St Eloi. Of the many battalions which had been involved the Northumberland Fusiliers had been reckoned to have given a good account of themselves and a number of official congratulations were received. On 23 April, St George's Day, after they had spent time resting and refitting, at a congratulatory dinner, medals

Strong shell proof shelters were constructed by the Germans for command centres, medical posts and troop accommodationbehind the lines at Hollebeke, near the canal. These show the large amount of work which has gone into them, they are also well camouflaged. Although the British identified them by aerial photographs, mainly by the pathmarks, they were not aware how strong they were until some were taken during fighting.

were presented to officers (five of whom got the Military Cross) and men (four Distinguished Conduct Medals and, later, seven Military Medals) for various deeds on 27 March. The Commanding Officer, Lieutenant Colonel W. H. Wild, was awarded the Distinguished Service Order and made a grant of 6d per man for the evening's celebrations.

The Northumberlands were soon to be back in the trenches, taking turns with other battalions in front of Wytschaete. The Messines Ridge sector was again a 'quiet' zone with troops carrying out routine duties of improving defences, fighting off occasional German raids and sheltering from spasmodic shell fire. During the last days of April 1916 German deserters from Spanbroekmolen and Messines gave indications that a large number of gas cylinders had been installed ready for an imminent major attack on the British lines in front of Wytschaete and Messines, held by the 3rd and 24th Divisions. The troops in front and rear positions were put on full gas alert and stood to. At 12.35am in the morning of 30 April, just behind the front line between Petite Douve Farm and Spanbroekmolen, the Germans

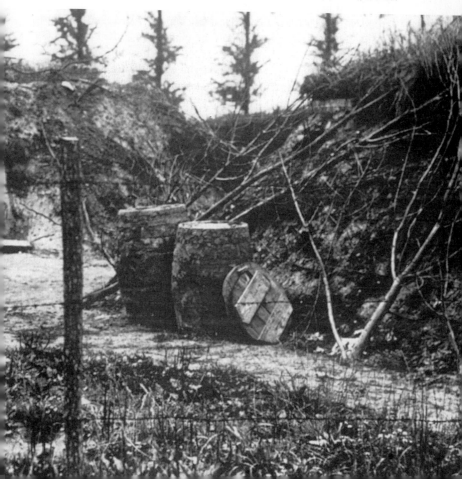

released from 4,000 cylinders clouds of a poisonous mixture of chlorine and phosgene, with infantry of the 211th and 212th Reserve Regiments following the gas cloud towards the British trenches. Unfortunately for the Germans the wind was fairly brisk and the gas clouds soon passed over the defenders who were then able to take off their masks and tackle the attackers. The Germans managed to take a small length of the British front trench in front of Spanbroekmolen from the 10th Royal Welch Fusiliers but were evicted within twenty minutes. Elsewhere along the line of attack the Germans made little headway and were soon back in their own trenches. By 4.30am, as the day dawned, the fighting was over and the front settled down to another quiet day. Five hundred and sixty two British had been killed or hurt by the gas, with 393 from other causes. After a day the course of the gas was evident on the ground as grass and crops were scorched and cattle died near Bailleul, well behind the fighting zone.

The Germans repeated the gas attack six weeks later, on 17 June, this time with a much stronger concentration of the poisonous clouds. The wind was light and the gas cloud was dense, moving very slowly across No Man's Land from Messines. The 1st North Staffordshires were badly affected by the gas but the cloud then drifted back to the German lines and few Germans emerged from behind their defences; those that did were soon prevented from approaching the British by rifle and machine gun fire and the attack petered out.

Chapter Four

1917. PLUMER'S PREPARATIONS

Plans for a major assault to push the Germans off the Messines Ridge had been hatched since the middle of 1915, when the commander of the Second Army which held this sector, General Sir Herbert Plumer, had considered that any plan to push the Germans back through Belgium must be preceded by their removal from this high ground. Until the ridge was in British hands any break-out from the Ypres Salient was deemed to be impossible as German artillery observation over the land between Ypres and the Passchendaele Ridge would deny the British any chance of success. In January 1916, before the planning for the Battle of the Somme was agreed, at a meeting of the British commanders, General Haig agreed with the views of Plumer and instructed him to begin preparations as the attack in Flanders might begin before the Somme battle. Plumer then stated that plans were already under way and 19 mines were currently being dug, with miners working their way deep underground towards the German lines. It was intended at this stage that a major attack on the Germans in Belgium would be launched in the summer of 1916, beginning with the clearing of the ridge, then a joint operation of a push from Ypres in

The spring of 1916: Germans outside their Unterstand or shelter, no. 19. At this time the British were drawing up plans for a large scale mining operation to remove the German front line strongpoints on the western side of Messines Ridge. Notice the German soldier wearing British puttees.

conjunction with the landing of two divisions on the coast near Middelkirke, in German hands. During the early months of 1916 this was to be the next major British offensive; however plans changed. The Battle of the Somme, which started on 1 July, was not over in the few days that had been presumed and all reserves and resources were sucked into that maelstrom. It was 7 July, whilst British troops were still being slaughtered in front of Ovillers, La Boisselle and other Somme villages still in German hands that General Haig decided that his Flanders operation could not proceed, and the Messines attack was called off.

General Plumer, though, knew that the right time for such an operation to take Messines Ridge would occur again and instead he continued with his plans. By this time the majority of the mines were at or nearing completion and almost a million pounds of ammonal, blastine and guncotton were being placed, ready for detonation beneath the Germans. The explosives were to sit there for almost a year, with mine tunnels and electric detonator systems checked and maintained constantly over this period.

The tunnels themselves had been triumphs of engineering and planning. The scheme to tunnel much deeper than had been carried out before, to depths of between 20 and 30 metres, had been inspired by Major John Norton Griffiths, who had been a civil engineering contractor before the war, and enthusiastically adopted by the Royal Engineers. The geological conditions were extremely difficult; much of the land at the base of the ridge, where the British lines were and from which tunnelling commenced, was water-bearing sand (named Kemmel Sand after the hill

Tunnellers working in much the same conditions as coal miners. Lighted candles and often canaries were taken into the shafts to give warning of the presence of dangerous gases.

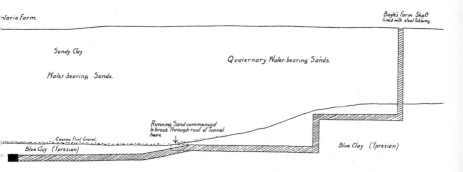

The mine to be exploded under the German strongpoint at Ontario Farm was begun 400 metres away at Boyle's Farm, a ruin just behind the British front line, on the Messines–Wulvergem road. The 171st Tunnelling Company, Royal Engineers, had to sink steel tubing down through the water-bearing sand to the blue clay before starting a horizontal gallery towards the German line. The gallery met with the sloping strata and resulted in a roof collapse: the tunnel was quickly sealed and then the gallery was dug deeper. The nature of the ground above the explosion when it was detonated by the Royal Engineers officers, Ellis and Daniell, of 171st Company, affected the nature of the disruption and unlike the other mines, which had some clay above and formed deep craters, the Ontario Farm mine resulted in the sandy ground rising into the air and falling back into the same place with no discernible crater but a muddy, steaming patch which bubbled gently for several days. Ontario Farm, its strongpoint and garrison had disappeared into the morass.

behind the British lines where it occurred at the surface and made dug-outs impossible) and alluvial clays and mines were liable to flood and collapse. Beneath these layers was a thick bed of very heavy Ypresian clay, which is similar to blue London clay. Tunnelling was hard work and progress was slow but the rigid nature of this strata enabled dry and fairly stable mines to be worked, although the length of time the tunnels were kept open due to the postponement lead to swelling of the clay and crushing of the support timbers, creating problems for the Engineers. The blue clay spoil from the mines had to be carefully disposed of above ground well away from the mines: its appearance, if spotted by German airmen or raiding troops, would negate the element of surprise and all advantage would be lost. The labour requirement for the scheme was high, six tunnelling companies of Royal Engineers (three British, two Canadian and one Australian, all with personnel drawn largely from mining and related industries who had been selected from their various infantry regiments) with numerous infantry carrying parties were engaged and, in an effort to speed up progress, a mechanical tunnelling machine, from the construction of the London Underground which had gone through the London clay, was brought over. The machine was found to be unreliable and could not exceed the rate achieved by the manual diggers 'clay kicking', lying on their backs and cutting the clay by working a spade with the feet. With a tunnel of standard dimensions 1.3 metres high and 0.7 wide, good progress, including timbering, was 0.3 metres (I foot) per hour. The boring machine was not withdrawn from the tunnel being worked towards Petit Bois; as it was stuck fast it was abandoned, and remains there to this day, some 20 metres below ground. By the time all the tunnels were complete the miners had driven a total of eight miles of galleries deep beneath the ground. The time the tunnellers spent in the mines was nerve-wracking as the risk of entrapment by roof fall or enemy camouflets was very high; listeners took turns to try and filter the sounds of their own workings from those of the Germans, sitting alone in the dark with a pair of geophones.

The Germans on the ridge had also been busy over 1916. They knew that the British would at some stage want to try and capture the high ground to prevent German observation over the ground in front of Ypres, and also suspected that Flanders might figure highly in British strategic thinking. Their suspicions were heightened with the increase in British activity - troop movements and traffic increases - opposite the ridge in the early part of 1917. Increasing their counter-mining (Quetshungen, or crushing operations) they fired camouflets, small

One of the surviving German bunkers in front of Messines, close to the cemetery. From here the Germans had excellent views over the British lines. No. 42 on map, page 135.

charges in mines designed to cause collapse in the British tunnels. Where underground conditions allowed they bored bown and channelled water into the subterranean workings; by this method they were successful in completely flooding the British mine under Petite Douve Farm, the only one of the series put out of action. The German engineers planning the abwehrminen or counter-mining, headed by Lieutenant-Colonel Füsslein, thought that they had destroyed most of the British workings, and reported that a British attack preceded by mine explosions was no longer possible.

They did, however, continue to improve their defences above ground. The position of the German front line was unusual in that, unlike other sectors where they had the forward line on or just behind a ridge (hinterhangstellungen), at Messines it lay on the forward slope. This meant that whilst they had complete observation over the British rear areas and the lines to the north at Ypres, it also allowed the British on Hill 63 and Kemmel Hill, 4,000 metres to the west, full observation over the front German line. Every detail of the front position could be watched; also the salient which Messines Ridge formed was liable to attack from three sides. Moreover the reverse, or eastern slope of the ridge, where it slopes down towards the River Lys, is slightly convex, hampering artillery observation over the support lines.

The front line position (Vorderstestellung) on the western slopes of the ridge consisted of shallow trenches – a main and support line with communications – behind a built-up breastwork of sandbags interspersed with reinforced concrete machine gun posts. This system, thinly manned by the Kampf-Truppen, or front line garrison, took in Petite Douve and Ontario Farms, the Spanbroekmolen spur, Peckham and Maedelstede Farms, Petit Bois and Croonart Wood. To the north of St. Eloi it ran up to Hill 60 then it continued to encircle Ypres.

On the crest of the ridge, running just in front of Messines and Wytschaete villages, ran the Second Line, the Höhen or Ridge Line, largely on the western side of the main road, the N365. Between these two lines was the Forward Zone, in which was a network of infantry fire trenches,the main one of which was Sonne (Sun) trench, machine gun posts at 50 metre intervals, trench mortars and shell proof concrete shelters. It was here that the German planners expected any British attack to grind to a halt. On the reverse, or rear slope, of the ridge the Germans had sited an intermediate line, or Zwischenstellung, named the Sehnen or chord line on account of the fact that it cut across the back of the salient like a bow string. Here were based the support troops or Bereitschaft-Truppen. The line ran past the hamlet of

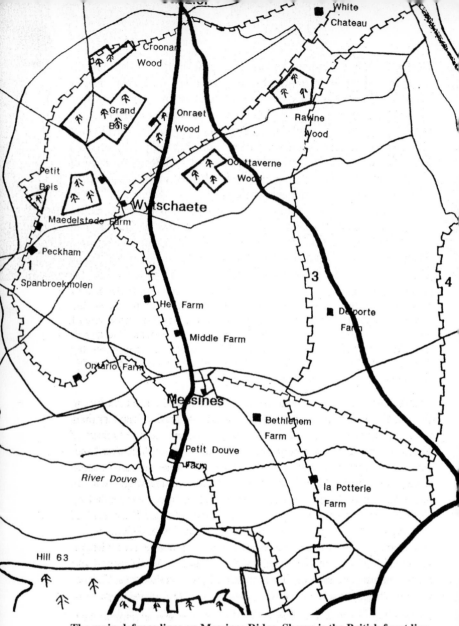

The main defence lines on Messines Ridge. Shown is the British front line, mainly on the lower ground at the foot of the hill. The German lines were not sited in their usual most favourable positions. The front line (1) and the Höhen (2) lines and the fighting zone between were in full view of the British on Hill 63, and Kemmel Hill, 4 kilometres to the west. German artillery observers and commanders behind the Intermediate (3) and Warneton (4) lines also had limited visibility over the ground in front.

Saxon officer of the 104th Infantry Regiment, of the 40th Division who held Messines for much of 1916 and 1917, in a forward trench on the western slope of the ridge. The trenches are shallow with raised breastworks consisting of earth behind barrels and boards. The trench also shows a utility rarely seen in British trenches, electric power for lighting in the bunkers and dugouts. The sign is a warning that the cable is dangerous and touching it is forbidden.

Oosttaverne and was subsequently named the Oosttaverne Line by the British. The Höhen and Sehnen lines joined just north of the Comines Canal, where they formed the Albrecht line, the second line in front of Ypres. At the rear of the ridge was sited the Third or Warneton Line, which ran north from Warneton then turned to cross the canal before Hollebeke. The whole of the defence system on the ridge was the responsibility of Gruppe Wytschaete, or XIX Corps, commanded by General von Laffert. His superiors were Crown Prince Rupprecht of Bavaria, commanding the Northern Group of Armies, and General Sixt von Armin, commanding the Fourth Army in whose area Gruppe Wytschaete was. Prince Rupprecht,with his Chief of Staff General von Kuhl, and advisors such as the German authority on defences, Colonel von Lossberg, considered that the positions on the forward slope were

German light railway carrying steel rails, fascines and aggregates from Wervick to the front at Messines for the construction of shell proof shelters.

One of the bunkers which still exist in Croonart Wood, no. 21 on map. Front line defence posts were constructed using pre-cast concrete blocks strengthened with interlocking steel bars, they were designed to shelter troops who could emerge when the shelling stopped.

not good and offered some advantage to the British. On 2 May 1917 a scheme was therefore put forward to evacuate the forward lines to the British and fall back to the rear of the ridge. The German divisional commanders strongly disagreed with the idea of withdrawal, and the artillery commander of Gruppe Wytschaete said that his artillery organisation was superior to the British and in the event of an artillery duel his guns would win.

It was therefore decided to further strengthen the defences on the ridge and increase the number of troops from three divisions (2nd, 40th and 204th) to four (with the 24th) in the trenches; two specially trained Eingreif or counter-attack divisions (35th and 3rd Bavarian, which had recently lost over 2,000 men at Arras) were brought in and artillery batteries and ammunition supplies were increased. As the front line divisions were worn out by artillery before the battle started two divisions were replaced by the 7th and 1st Guard Reserve Divisions.

The six divisions the Gruppe Wytschaete commander, von Laffert, had to defend the ridge amounted to 75,000 men, with a total of 630 artillery pieces ranging from field guns, some of which were dug-in as anti-tank measures, to heavy howitzers. He had been promised some extra aeroplanes to boost his air force but in the event these were delayed and arrived too late to be of any assistance.

The front line divisions were instructed to fight a mobile defence; if the front battalions had to fall back they would find the support battalions behind ready to launch an immediate counter-attack. The only exception to the mobile defence system was to be the knoll of Spanbroekmolen, which was to be retained at all costs.

At the same time as the Germans were re-organising their defences for the expected onslaught, the British were finalising their plans and arrangements. As the tunnellers of the Royal Engineers continued underground, maintaining the completed mines and finishing off others, other Engineers were busy on the surface. The main line railway system from the ports of Calais, Dunkirk and Boulogne was increased by a total of 115 miles of track to bring supplies closer towards the front; the network of light gauge and trench railways was increased so that large quantities of ammunition for the heavy batteries could be delivered direct and the large amounts of other ammunition, engineer stores and general supplies could be stockpiled in the correct locations to be ready when needed. The ever-increasing number of men in the rear zones needed accommodation, so numerous camps of wooden Nissen huts, tents and tunnelled shelters had to be produced. Many of the shelters towards the front, for machine gun crews, telephone centres, medical centres, battalion headquarters, battery commanders and advanced ammunition supplies needed to be shell or splinter proof; many of these shelters were built, some of which were of reinforced concrete, a system until then not widely used by the British.

Saxon soldiers of the 134th Infantry Regiment, 40th Division, holding the trenches on top of the ridge. They are obviously fairly relaxed, as this is still a relatively quiet area. These troops also have the security of strong concrete shelters, Mannschafts Eisen Beton Unterstands (MEBU), which had recently been constructed by the Bavarian Reserve Pioneer Company 13, who carried out much of the fortification work around Messines.

Although a 'quiet' area, both sides carried out regular if spasmodic shelling of the other side's trenches. These Saxons have just emerged from their concrete shelters and started to clear up the damage after British shelling. Whereas the trench and earthworks are badly damaged the bunkers are untouched.

Infantry working parties were used to dig a large number of assembly trenches, immediately behind the front and support lines. These were marked out with green tape, not visible to the Germans, during the night by Engineer liaison officers, with the infantry working through the following night to dig the trenches and lay trench boards.

The road system leading to the battle area was upgraded to allow for the great increase in motor and troop movements, with steam-powered road rollers working as close as 1,500 metres to the front line, and protected crossings were placed over water and telephone lines, with bridges built to allow heavy artillery and tanks to cross streams and rivers. In anticipation of shell damage and to extend roads into the captured territory, stockpiles of road stone and planks were built up at dumps. The supply of water for men and horses was seen as being crucial to the operation and much work was expended in ensuring its availability. Mains pipes were laid where possible, with storage tanks of metal and canvas set up; some streams were dammed, barges on the Lys were used as reservoirs of chemically sterilized water, and barrels and petrol tins collected for forward supplies. Volumes of up to 600,000 gallons per day were supplied to the Messines front, and mobile water lorries and carts and pipe dumps were arranged to enable the water supply to be rapidly expanded across the devastated area and Horrocks Sets - chemical testing apparatus to check for poison in the water from wells on the ridge – were supplied to R.E. forward headquarters. In the event these arrangements for water were very successful, with some troops having water brought up within minutes of fighting their way into their objectives in the German lines. In some instances the first wave troops carried water tins to guarantee supplies. The 2nd Otago Infantry Battalion of the New Zealanders, who stormed Messines, stockpiled their water in the front line German trench and left it under armed guard whilst they proceeded up the hill to the village. The labour requirement for all these tasks and preparations put a strain on available manpower and by the time of the assault over 30,000 men per day were working to make sure all was completed on time.

The villages of Messines and Wytschaete, and the roads and farms, were already in ruins after two and a half years of being shelled, and the fields and woods had been stripped of most of their greenery. The forthcoming battle was to ensure that any remaining buildings would be demolished as, in the middle of May, the British started the preparatory bombardments of the German defences, headquarters, gun batteries and supply dumps. A total of 2,266 guns and howitzers, ranging in size from 18 pounder field guns to 15 inch howitzers, had been assembled in the build-up, more than three times the German's artillery. A major target was the German artillery batteries, and many of the heavy howitzers were devoted to this, with fire being directed by artillery-direction pilots who flew over the German lines. The batteries were assailed with high explosive during the day and gas at night to ensure the gun crews had to keep on their gas masks and therefore get little sleep. To starve and exhaust the front line troops all roads and tracks were shelled at night, and the defence lines were continually shelled to eliminate strongpoints and destroy the rows of barbed wire and trenches. The concrete shelters, machine gun posts and command centres of the front lines, the Oosttaverne and Warneton Lines, were all targeted with howitzers both during the day and the night. The remnants of Messines and Wytschaete, which were known to be well defended strongpoints, were given special treatment with high explosive and gas to minimise their potential threat to the attackers. Gas shells were a mixture of lacrymatory or tear gas, designed to irritate the eyes and hamper sight and the use of masks, and lethal gas to kill. During the week leading up to the start of the offensive the British artillery fired over $3^{1}/_{2}$ million shells at the Germans on and around Messines Ridge.

The German batteries fired back at the British artillery in retaliation and this counter-battery fire had some success, but not enough to reduce the British fire, the Germans also deliberately did not use some of their batteries in order to maintain the secrecy of their positions.

Over 3½ million artillery shells were fired by the British before the Battle of Messines. The Germans retaliated, and the shelling continued throughout that battle and the rest of 1917, the German offensive of spring 1918 and the British Final Advance in September. Of the many millions of shells, some which did not explode are still lying around in a very dangerous condition. The one above is on the site of the German front trench, now a cow pasture on the western slope. Shells which are found or ploughed up are collected by the Belgian Army and taken to Houthulst Forest near Ypres where, after the gas shells are separated, they are exploded.

Knowing that the Germans still had some heavy artillery in reserve the British on several occasions started 'creeping' and 'box' bombardments to make the Germans believe an infantry assault was about to begin. This also served to rehearse and modify phased timings for batteries.

The Royal Flying Corps, whose numbers of bombers, fighters and reconnaissance planes were boosted by the Royal Naval Air Service, had control of the skies over the ridge, a situation which was unusual for them as they were generally outclassed by superior machines. The RFC made full use of their period of mastery of the air in the days before the battle began, directing gun batteries, photographing defences and damage inflicted, bombing transport lines and supply depots and denying German flyers the use of the skies, downing 44 German machines in the last five days with a loss of 10 British planes. The flyers had luck with the weather; as May turned into June the fine weather with clear skies allowed good observation and photography so the results of the bombardments could be ascertained and any new works or movements identified.

During the weeks before the attack was timed to begin the infantry also played their part in wearing down the Germans, taking prisoners to identify regiments so troop movements could be monitored and inflicting as much damage as possible by carrying out series of raids (sometimes officially referred to as 'enterprises') into the German front and support trenches. The forays, generally, but not always, with the assistance of artillery which could isolate trench sections with a box barrage, into the German lines were carried on all along the front, mainly at night but sometimes during daylight hours. Some raids yielded good information and intelligence from interrogated prisoners but there were dangers and the success rate was not always 100%. The Australians, inveterate raiders, reported a number of failures and losses of their men.

The 13th Cheshires of the 25th Division raided the German lines in front of Messines at 11.35pm on 16 May to determine the condition of the front trenches and the degree with which they were manned. They found the front trench unoccupied except for one man who was bayonetted in the struggle; shell holes between the front and support lines were full of Germans however and the Cheshires could not go any further after they met with solid resistance. They stayed in the German front trench for 20 minutes before retiring and on returning found Second Lieutenant Malone to be missing. A search party went back over No Man's Land and found him to be caught up in the German wire, opposite a machine gun position. The party tried to extricate him, during which attempt he was wounded by the machine gun. Unable to free him from the wire the party had to withdraw as the sun came up. Later in the morning Second Lieutenant Malone was seen to be taken into the German front trench by a party of their stretcher bearers. The 10th Royal Warwickshires reported a similar story after 21 men under Second Lieutenant Butcher raided the northern corner of Croonart Wood at 1.30am on 28 May:

'The raid was not an unqualified success. Just as the raiders had got through the wire and the barrage opened, enemy were seen moving along what was thought to be an unused piece of trench. As they threatened to cut the raiders off they attacked them at once. Generally handicapped by shellholes filled with water; after an exchange of shots and bombs the men withdrew. 2nd Lieutenant Butcher and 5 men wounded but all were brought back to our lines'.

The report also stated that four Germans had been killed but no prisoners taken.

The Irishmen of the 16th Division opposite Wytschaete were carrying out raids almost every night, some of them very large operations. One of the larger ones, involving 12 officers, 300 men and 12 Royal Engineers was carried out by the 2nd Dublins on the night of 27 May. The Dublins captured 30 Germans and killed 50, and took a lot of papers and maps which were found to yield valuable information. Reports of other raids were often congratulatory, the 6th Royal Irish, opposite Wytschaete, recorded a raid on the night of 5 June:

'A most successful undertaking, 21 prisoners of 4th Grenadier Regiment, from which inestimable information gained. Casualties. Captain J. E. Day, died of wounds, also 6 men killed, 7 missing, 66 wounded'.

Most of the raid reports confirmed the poor condition of the German front line, as reported by the 8th Royal Inniskilling Fusiliers after their raid on the German trenches they named Nail Trench and Nail Switch, between Petit Bois and Grand Bois, at 10.25 pm just two nights before the main offensive:

'Information concerning GERMAN FRONT LINE.

Generally this hardly exists and there was no sign of occupation, none of the Officers who entered the front line saw any Germans. A certain number of dug-outs were found but they had not been occupied and in some cases were waterlogged. There is practically no wire except a few scattered concertinas and there is a certain amount of wire near the willows about [map reference] N.18.d,00.72.The 'going' in No Man's Land was found to be quite good. NAG and NAIL ROW are practically obliterated and unoccupied.

Information concerning NAIL SWITCH.

At the North End this trench was found to be in better order than was expected and there were still dug-outs which are intact. The Southern End of this Line is badly damaged and was difficult to recognise. The wire in front of the whole line has practically disappeared. All the prisoners were obtained from this line nine of them issuing from one dug-out, five of whom were killed in returning to our front line.

Number of prisoners taken. Four arrived at our front line.

No machine gun emplacements were found which were not already blown in.

Casualties. 1 Officer wounded. 13 O.R. wounded

The morale of the prisoners appeared to be distinctly poor.'

The New Zealanders were particularly interested in the German defences at Petite Douve Farm, which was in an important position for their part in the forthcoming offensive and was a potential trouble spot on account of its position and the field of fire from any machine guns there. The original plan had called for a mine to be exploded beneath the farm but, as this plan had been thwarted by the Germans, the New Zealanders wanted to see the extent of the threat. At 3.30 in the afternoon of 5 June a party of the 2nd New Zealand Rifle Brigade, under Lieutenant Manning and 2nd Lieutenant Pattrick entered the trenches around the farm, which was found to be not heavily manned. Two concrete dug-outs were found, one was examined by Lieutenant Manning and Corporals Calder and Lecky then blown up, the other was examined by Sergeant Scully, and valuable information gained,

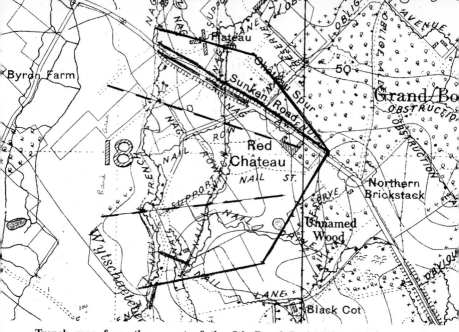

Trench map from the report of the 8th Royal Inniskilling Fusiliers showing the trenches raided, Nail Trench and Nail Switch, between the broken lines. The solid lines mark the extent of the protective artillery barrage. Byron Farm was the raid headquarters and report centre.

although one officer, Captain S.A. Atkinson, was killed and Second Lieutenant Pattrick and two soldiers wounded.

The British were pleased with the information from the raids about the poor condition of the German defences after the repeated shelling, although they were not sure what to make of the information that the front trenches were only lightly manned. This was in accordance with new German principles of defence: the front trench was not important but the ground between this and the second line formed the forward zone and this was where the machine guns and strongpoints were.

The trench raids, even the smaller operations, required a lot of planning and co-ordination. An example of the organisation, together with report and awards to some participants, is given by the Operation Orders for the 9th Royal Welch Fusiliers instructing a raid on Oblige Trench and Oblige Switch, in the gap between Grand Bois and Croonart Wood, on the night of 4 June.

While the raids, interrogation of prisoners and aerial reconnaissances kept up a constant flow of information, Plumer and his planners were finalising their strategy for the assault on the ridge. As this was seen as being a minor, but important, precursor to the main attack which had the object of breaking out of the Ypres salient and

SECRET.

OPERATION ORDERS
by
Lieut.-Colonel L.F. Smeathman, M.C.
Commanding 9th (S) Bn. Royal Welch Fusiliers.   4/6/17.

1. INFORMATION.
   "C" Company 9th. R.W.F. will carry out a raid on the enemy lines
   on the 5th. inst.   Two Companies of the 56th. Brigade will, at the
   same time, raid on the immediate left of "C" Company. Touch will
   be maintained with these Companies throughout the operation.
   There will be no raiding party on the right of "C" Company.

2. OBJECTIVE.
   OBLIGE SWITCH from O.13.a.50.82 to O.7.c.65.30.

3. INTENTION.
   To capture (not to kill) Germans.

4. FORMATION.
   "C" Coy: will attack with 3 platoons in one wave (1 line of men
   only) and 1 platoon in the second wave.   The second wave will be
   on the right rear of the 1st. wave.

5. BARRAGE.
   The barrage will open on the enemy front line at ZERO, will lift
   100 yards at ZERO plus 04, remain there for 2 minutes (to ZERO
   plus 06) lift 100 yards and remain there till ZERO plus O.10, lift
   100 yards and remain there until ZERO plus O.25.
   The Objective will probably not be able to be assaulted until
   ZERO plus O.10, but if the barrage allows, men will get into the
   Objective before this lift takes place.

6. ZERO.
   ZERO hour will be notified later but the Company will be in position
   by 2-30 p.m.

7. TIME IN OBJECTIVE.
   The Objective will be reached at ZERO plus O.11 and will be cleared
   at ZERO plus 16.   This will give 9 minutes for the Company to
   withdraw to our own lines.

8. SIGNALS.
   Two Very Lights will be fired in quick succession from our own
   Front line by 2/Lieut. S.G. MANDERS at ZERO plus 16 as a signal
   for withdrawal.   At the same time a Bugle will be blown, under
   the orders of 2/Lieut. MANDERS in our own front line, and two
   Very pistol lights will be sent up by 2/Lieut. E.O. ROBERTS in
   the enemy lines.

9. DRESS.
   Coats will not be worn, otherwise Drill Order.

10 Equipment.
   One bomb per man will be carried in the trousers pocket but the
   greatest care will be taken that these are only used as a means
   of defence and that they will not be thrown except in exceptional
   circumstances. No identifications will be carried on the man and
   men must be cautioned that, in the unlikely event of their being
   captured, they must on no account give any information beyond their
   names. Bombers, in bombing sections, will carry 5 bombs each in
   the haversack, rifle grenadiers will not carry Rifle grenades.
   Lewis Gunners will carry gun and 8 magazines only.   Smoke
   bombs (1 per Section) will be carried. These will be used a make
   a smoke barrage when withdrawing from the enemy trench.

11 OFFICERS.
   2/Lieut. E.O. ROBERTS and 2/Lieut. D.W. THOMAS.

12. WITHDRAWAL.
   Upon withdrawal from the enemy line, the 1st. wave will withdraw
   through the 2nd wave to our own lines and men will return down
   POPPY LANE and assemble in the NEW RESERVE LINE independently.

REPORT ON RAID.

1. The raid on the whole was a great success.
2. A Copy of Battalion Orders for the raid is attached.
3. The objective was easily reached.
4. 37 prisoners passed by Battalion Headquarters but it is known that a considerable number of the prisoners captured by this Battalion were cleared down CHICORY TRENCH and thus went through the 56th Brigade.
5. It is impossible to say at present really how many casualties have occurred. The following are known :-
   - 1 Officer seriously wounded. (2/Lt. D.W. THOMAS.)
   - 2 Men Killed. One of these was brought in.
   - 9 Men Wounded.
   - 1 Man Missing., but a party of 1 N.C.O. and 2 men have, it is thought, found him in "NO MANS LAND" and are waiting to bring him in to-night.
6. No gap occurred between the Battalion on the Left and this Battalion, but a gap occurred between the two platoons of this Battalion.
7. The gap was caused by a 4.5 in. Howitzer Battery shooting short.
8. The Barrage was not so good as that put up three days ago.
9. No difficulty was experienced in following the barrage, the alignment of which was good but pauses (not gaps) occurred in it.
10. The Front Line German Trench is almost demolished. Three dug-outs were found in it, two of which were concrete and contained Germans. The OBLIGE SWITCH LINE contained dug-outs and was in fairly good condition.
11. The Wire was no obstacle anywhere.
12. One German Machine Gun fired from the NAGS NOSE; position not identified but thought to be on the edge of the GRAND BOIS. One German Machine Gun was destroyed in a dug-out in the NAGS NOSE by two Sergeants of this Battalion.
13. Germans only put up a fight in two places.
14. No Germans were found on watch; they were all in dug-outs or close against the walls.
15. The enemy shelled his own Front Line on the Right and Very Lights XXXX (RED) were fired by him in a Northerly direction from the NAGS NOSE.
16. 15 Germans are known to have been killed with the bayonet.

                        (Sgd) L.F. SMEATHMAN,   Lieut.-Colonel,

5/6/17.   Commanding 9th (S) Bn. Royal Welch Fusiliers.

O.C. 9th R.W.Fusiliers.

       Major General SHUTE wishes to convey his congratulations and thanks to the Battalion for the part they took in the Raid to-day.   The result was splendid.

O.C. 9th R.W.Fusiliers.

       Convey to "C" Company, 9th R.W.Fus, Brigadiers Hearty Congratulations on excellent work this afternoon.

2/Lieut. Douglas Walter Thomas. awarded Military Cross for the
following act :-
"During a raid on the enemy lines in the WYTSCHAETE Area
"on the 5th June 1 17, set a magnificent example to all
"N.C.O's and men.
" It is known that he shot two Germans and stunned
"another with the butt of his revolver.
"He was seriously wounded. This Officer has on numerous
"previous occasions done most excellent patrol work in the
"enemy line."

16680 Sergt. C. Bannister. awarded Distinguished Conduct Medal, for
the following act :- -
"During a raid on the enemy lines in the WYTSCHAETE Sector
"on the 5th June 1917, this Sergt, was in command of a
"platoon, the duty of which was to guard the right flank
"of the Battalion.
" Owing to his able-leadership, this platoon thoroughly
"performed its allotted task.
" This Sergt., with Sergt. Evans then, with a complete
"disregard of his own safety, attacked and destroyed a
"German Machine Gun in a concrete emplacement, which was
"firing on the flank of the raiding party.
" his plucky action undoubtedly saved many lives.

9366 Sergt. XXXXXXXX Evans. T. awarded Military Medal for the
following act :-
"During a raid on the enemy trenches in the WYTSCHAETE
"Sector on the 5th June 1917, he, in company with Sergt.
"Bannister, and with a complete disregard of his personal
"safety, attacked and destroyed a German Machine Gun
"which was causing much trouble to the Right flank of the
"raiding party."

33463 Cpl. Bonsall. H. awarded Military Medal for the following act:-
"This N.C.O., during a raid on the German Lines in the XX
"WYTSCHAETE Sector on the 5th June 1917, displayed the
"greatest ability in leading his section. It is established
"beyond doubt that he killed two Germans with the bayonet
"and captured 5 more personally."

16652 Pte. Siviter. E. awarded the Military Medal for the
following act :-
"During a raid on the enemy trenches in the WYTSCHAETE
"Sector on the 5th June 1917, he performed numerous acts
"of great gallantry.
" He continuously left our own line to help and dress
"wounded in spite of heavy Machine Gun fire from the enemy.
" He ultimately crawled out in full daylight up to the
"enemy front line to a Lance Corporal who was wounded and
"gave him water.
" He has previously been recommended 4 times, but so
"far, has not had any recognition of his most valuable
"services."

13505 Pte. Weeks. F., awarded the Military Medal for the following
act :-
"During a raid on the enemy trenches in the WYTSCHAETE
"Area on the 5th June 1917, this man was the last to leave
"the enemy lines. He found a wounded Lance Corporal who he
"could not carry, came in and reported and returned to the
"Lance Corporal, across NO MAN's LAND in broad daylight
"and in spite of heavy enemy Machine Gun fire.
" He also assisted in the saving of a badly wounded
"Officer on the same occasion."

13367 Pte. Jones. T. awarded xxx a Bar to his Military Medal for
for the following act :-
"When 2/Lieut. D.W. Thomas was badly wounded during a
"raid on the enemy lines in the WYTSCHAETE Sector on the
"5th June 1917, this man, in spite of heavy enemy
"XXXXXXXXXXX fire from Machine Guns, and with complete
"disregard of his own personal safety dashed out from
"our own lines and brought 2/Lieut. THOMAS in.
"On four other occasions during the same raid he brought
"in wounded men at great personal risk.
He had already been awarded a Military Medal.

clearing the Belgian coast up to Ostend, the effect on other operations had to be considered, and the scheme underwent several modifications before the plan was finalised. Initial plans were for the Spanbroekmolen spur, from Ontario Farm to Peckham, to be captured before the main attack on the ridge. The objective was then to be only the near slope and the main defence line, the Höhenstellung, on the crest, including Messines village, to deny the Germans observation over the Flanders plain and the land to the east of Ypres. Wytschaete and the rear slope of the ridge was to be taken on the following day. Thus the ridge would be taken in a three day operation, and on the same three days attacks would be made further north from Boesinge to take the Pilkem Ridge, to be followed immediately by the landing of a force on the Belgian coast. It was eventually decided that the Messines-Wytschaete ridge and the area behind St. Eloi should be won before any of the other operations could begin, and the three days allotted to this was compressed into one half day, to begin at dawn on 7 June. As the time neared, thought was given to the possibility of a German withdrawal from the front line on the forward slope of the hill to the crest itself or even the Sehnen or Oosttaverne Line (which was precisely what the Germans themselves had contemplated and rejected). This would render the mines, by now mostly ready and primed beneath the German front line, redundant, so the idea of blowing the mines the day before the main assault was considered; however it was decided to stick to the timetable.

The final plan was for the explosion of the 19 mines beneath the front line (one under the Petite Douve Farm strongpoint had been abandoned when the Germans caused it to flood, and two doubles further south, opposite Ploegsteert Wood, were outside the revised area and not used), the firing of the mines to coincide with a massive artillery bombardment of front, intermediate and rear targets. Nine infantry divisions, assisted by 72 of the latest model tanks, the Mark IV, which was making its first appearance, and a massed machine gun barrage, were allocated objectives to be taken in waves: selected battalions were to cross No Man's Land as the mines went up and take the front line trenches, to be succeeded by battalions passing through to the next line, Sonne trench. On reaching and taking this line an immediate attack was to be launched by fresh troops on the first trenches of the crest (Höhen) line. At this stage a two hour wait was scheduled to allow the gains to be consolidated before the rear trenches of the line were tackled. This stage was to be the most important as this line was to be retained against any possible German counter-attack. A

Tanks moving up to the front at Messines.

further halt then allowed heavy and field gun batteries to come further forward before the final objective, the Oosttaverne Line, was assaulted and taken.

Each of the objectives - which corresponded to German trenches – were identified on maps as coloured lines; Red and Blue Lines on the forward slope and the main objective, on the crest, the Black Line with some outposts in front being the Black Dotted Line. The final objective, the Oosttaverne Line, was nominated the Green Line. The divisions directly opposite the crest of the ridge had a higher number of trenches to tackle and cross and had a secondary system of colours: the 25th Division, on the northern side of Messines village, had nine trench lines to overcome before reaching the crest and each of these were given colours as names; Yellow, Grey, Brown and others.

Divisions prepared themselves for the forthcoming event. Officers from the 16th (Irish) Division had a formal dinner at the Hospice in Locre on the evening of 4 June, Lieutenant-Colonel Buckley of 7th Leinsters proposed the health of the 16th Division in the coming offensive and replied to the speech given by the Nationalist MP, William Redmond. Redmond, a staunch advocate of Home Rule, had just given what was destined to be his last speech.

The privates and other ranks of the Irish battalions were also in celebratory mood; noticing that the heavy and field guns of the artillery were draped in green (netting with leaves as camouflage, still a novel device), were delighted and sang a variation of one of their favourite songs:

'so if by chance we all advance to Whitesheet and Messines,

they'll learn our guns that straffed the Huns
were wearing of the green'.

During the day and evening of 6 June, as the first rain for some time fell heavily, the Irish, English, Welsh, New Zealand and Australian troops in the training and resting camps set off for their assembly trenches, in accordance with carefully calculated timetables. About 80,000 troops filed along cross-country tracks and down the long communication trenches which had been produced by the Canadians in 1915 and 1916, and still bore their names: Medicine Hat Trail, Beaver, Calgary Avenue, P&O Trench. The Australians, on their way from camps around Pont de Nieppe, approached through Ploegsteert Wood as the Germans were bombarding the wood with gas shells (knowing the gas would be slow to disperse in the trees) and about 500 men were killed or disabled.

Eventually all the troops were in their assembly positions all along the British front and trenches immediately behind. In the dark smoking and noise was forbidden. All present were instructed to lie down to prevent being thrown off their feet by the ground tremors expected from the mines. Zero hour – 3.10 am – had been carefully chosen as $1^1/_2$ hours before dawn, and a visibility of 100 metres had been estimated as the first light glimmered. Troops and onlookers on vantage points at Hill 63 and Kemmel Hill waited nervously as the minutes ticked away. Later German accounts relate how nightingales could be heard singing in the remains of the woods as the almost full moon shone in the clear sky.

German officers with camouflaged trench periscope. As the British were preparing for the offensive the Germans were watching the build-up of arms and men: although they knew the attack was imminent they could not guess the actual date it was to start.

Chapter Five

1917. MAGNUM OPUS

At 3.10 am on 7 June 1917 the result of nearly two years tunnelling, and all the painstaking and meticulous arranging and planning, suddenly became visually obvious. The nineteen mines erupted in gigantic sheets of orange flame and earth as clouds of dust and smoke

The battle of Messines resulted in the whole of the objectives aimed at being attained in one day. This contour map covers the whole battle area, the black line on the left showing the original British position, and the dotted line on the right shows the line at the end of the same day. The scale can be judged from the fact that the distance from Messines to Wulvergehm is about two miles.

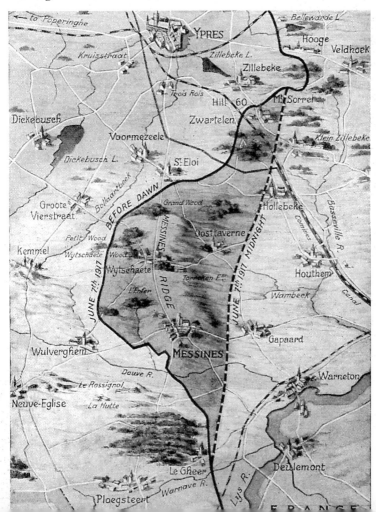

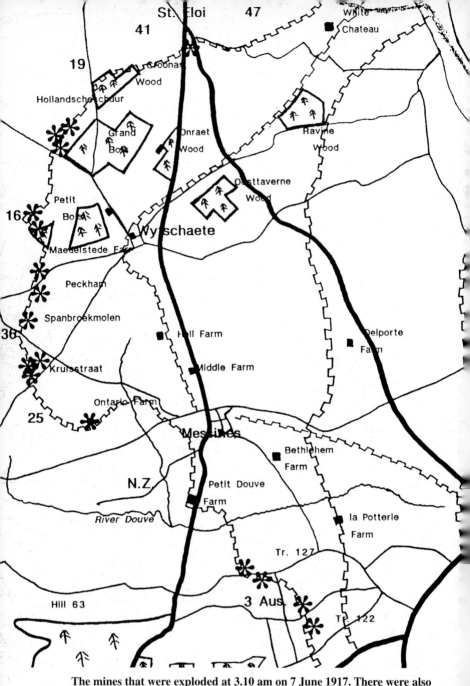

The mines that were exploded at 3.10 am on 7 June 1917. There were also two further north, at The Caterpillar and Hill 60. The attacking divisions, the leading battalions of which went over No Man's Land as the mines went up, are shown.

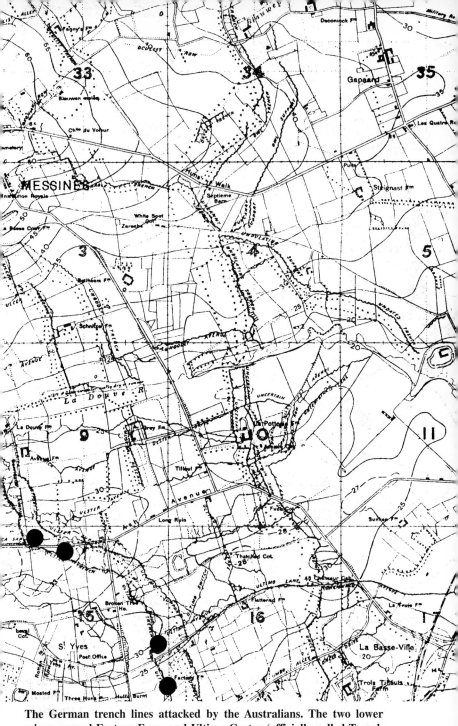

The German trench lines attacked by the Australians. The two lower mines, named Factory Farm and Ultimo Crater (officially called Trench 122 Right and Left) were to protect the flank of the attack. After the front line was overcome the next objective was Ungodly Trench and Bethlehem Farm in square 3. The Oosttaverne Line runs down the centre, in squares 34, 4 and 10.

Modern photograph, with Messines Church on the ridge, of the ground over which the 38th, 39th and 40th Australians attacked, stretching from lower left to upper right. In the foreground is the Petite Douve river which was crossed on portable bridges, beyond this was the German front and support trenches. The road on the left is the Ploegsteert–Messines road.

shot upwards and outwards. All along the front and for miles away the force of the explosions shook the earth. The shock was felt in London and in Lille, 20 kilometres away, the Professor of Geology at Lille University, M. Barrois, thought an earthquake had occurred, he dressed hurriedly in case of an after-shock and saw panic-stricken German soldiers running in the streets. For many German soldiers, those in the front lines, there was not the possibility of panicking or running as they were evaporated by the mine explosions or buried by the fall-out, others along the front trenches were rendered incapable of fighting as the tremendous shock paralysed and demoralized them.

As the deafening bellow of the explosions was reverberating around the countryside another great roar opened up as the whole of the massed artillery (2,230 guns and howitzers, with 700 machine guns and 428 mortars) began a sustained bombardment of important centres, communications and gun batteries. The planners had estimated a period of 20 seconds for the mine debris to fall back to earth. More difficult to predict was the amount of dust and smoke from the mines and countless shells falling on the German lines.

At the southern end of the ridge the 3rd Australian Division, the men going into battle for the first time and most having just reached their own front line due to the gas shelling in Ploegsteert Wood, left their trenches and started across No Man's Land. Their role in what they termed the 'Magnum Opus' was to attack northeastwards, those on the left had to cross the River Douve and portable bridges had been provided for this. They found that the Bavarians in the front trench had been very badly affected by the shelling and the mine explosions; very little resistance was met with and when the Australians arrived at the German trenches they found signs of panic and pandemonium. Rifles, ammunition, food and personal belongings were littered around as the garrison fled or surrendered willingly. One notable exception was a

80

Shattered remains of a German dugout, taken after the attack of 7 June 1917.

lone machine gunner in The Beak, an angle of front line trench where it crossed the Messines road, the N365. The machine gunner fired on the Tasmanians crossing the Douve until Lieutenant Crosby and a small group of men bombed him into submission.

On the right flank of the Australians, and of the whole attacking force, were some German positions in safe trenches outside of the front line. Machine guns here caused some casualties but these were dealt with by an arranged group with grenades and mortars. As dawn broke the Australians were in possession of all their first objectives and

Tranquil today: the mine crater which was officially named 'Trench 122 Left' removed a German strongpoint in their front line. The Australians of the 33rd Battalion who took the crater suffered casualties from German machine gunners beyond the rim until the crew were silenced by a light trench mortar. The crater was later known as 'Ultimo Crater' on account of a communication trench that led from it.

One of the two German bunkers in the New Zealand Memorial Park. These were on Uhlan Trench, the front line, and were known to the New Zealanders who had watched their construction.

began to consolidate their gains and await the arrival of their next wave while the New Zealanders on their left took Messines village. Just after 5am the second wave left the new line and made their way up the south slope of the hill. After capturing their first trench and Schnitzel Farm (the cemetery there is now known as Bethlehem Farm West) their objective was Ungodly Trench, a continuation of the crest line, the main objective of the day, together with the ruins of Bethlehem Farm just behind it. It was expected that Bethlehem Farm would be a well defended strongpoint and some resistance would be given. Infantry and a machine gun of the 9th Bavarian Regiment, on the roof of a concrete pill box at the farm, fired on the Australians until Captain F. Fairweather and three men worked their way behind to find the Bavarians either ready to surrender or had fled. Fairweather used the machine gun to fire on the fleeing Germans, by now sheltering in shell holes behind the farm. The Australians pressed on past the farm and in the field beyond found a field gun whose crew they shot and then another gun which had just been abandoned. The Australian 3rd Division dug in, using shovels found at the farm, content that they had carried out their part in the morning's work, the main battle for the crest of the ridge, but knowing that the Germans could counter-attack at any time.

The New Zealanders were also pleased that their part in the first stage had gone well. The 1st Rifle Brigade were not sure what to expect at the strongpoint at Petite Douve Farm, where the planned mine had been flooded. The resistance they met there was from a few isolated

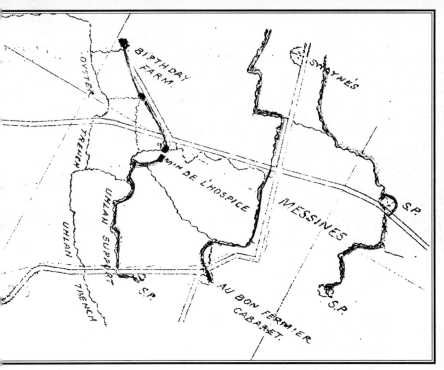

The map from the Operation orders for the New Zealanders attacking Messines village showing shaded the 1st, 2nd and 3rd objectives.

groups in and around the farm ruins and this was soon quashed. The front line running north from the farm, roughly parallel to the main road, was named Ulna Trench. The garrison here put up some fight before giving in and 40 prisoners were taken, 12 of them by one soldier, Corporal H.J. Jeffrey, who first silenced their machine gun then forced them to emerge from their dug-out with a grenade. Uhlan Trench, the front line directly in front of Messines village and on part of which the New Zealand Memorial Park now sits, was a strong line with clear views over the ground the attackers of the 1st and 3rd Rifles of the 3rd Brigade had to traverse. They crossed No Man's Land and the Steenbeck with little difficulty and captured the concrete pill boxes now in the Park, reporting that their 'troops kept very close to barrage, enemy had no time to man his parapet'. The position of these two pill boxes was known as the New Zealanders had watched them being built over May, giving regular progress reports in their daily Intelligence Summaries.

The 1st Otago Infantry Battalion, of the 2nd Brigade, and the 1st Canterbury on its right, had what was considered a particularly tough part of the line to win. They knew the ground in front of them well, having been in the front line here on and off since mid-March when they relieved the 13th Royal Irish Rifles and 9th Royal Irish Fusiliers. The leading two Companies, under Captains C. Molloy and J. Thompson, took the first lines with ease; and began to deal with the known strongpoints. The Moulin de l'Hospice was an observation post and machine gun position and a party went forward to tackle it. The mill was surrounded before the machine guns could come into action and the 20 occupants taken prisoner. The site of one the mill buildings is now the Rotunda of the New Zealand Memorial to the Missing in the entrance to Messines Ridge Cemetery, and the Cross of Sacrifice is on the site of the mill itself.

At Birthday Farm the German machine gunners of the Jäeger Regiment just managed to get their gun into action when snipers of the Otagos, carrying out a carefully rehearsed plan, covered the machine gun post while troops with hand and rifle grenades rushed it. Thirty prisoners came out, the Otagos reported that the Jäegers had only taken over the positions hours before the attack and were mainly very young men.

The Otago Battalion reported their successes to headquarters at 4.20 am, with a prize haul of a total of six officers, 155 troops, nine machine guns and three trench mortars, with two field guns, from their sector of the front line trenches

Once the trenches on the near slope had been consolidated other New Zealand troops passed through to take their main prize - the remains of Messines. Dawn had not yet broken and with the heavily shell-cratered ground the officers had to

S. Frickleton VC

check their direction. Battalions were entering the village from the west and the south, trying to push the Germans of the 18th Bavarian Regiment, who had only taken over from the Saxons the previous day, out eastwards. The fight for the rubble of the village was very patchy, many Germans were hiding in the maze of underground bunkers and fortified cellars the German engineers had produced. The 2nd Otago worked their way into the edge of the village and established a signal station to send messages to commanders in the rear. Captain Bremner MC advanced with some troops to assist the 2nd Canterbury who were to play a major part in clearing the village, while some men assisted in mopping up the remains of resistance and the German stragglers and stubborn defenders who were sniping and hurling grenades from within the ruins. The 3rd Rifle Battalion silenced resistance with bomb and bayonet, reporting 'a considerable amount of fighting in Messines, but enemy was disorganised'. Prominent in the action was Lance Corporal Samuel Frickleton, who ran through the British barrage to rush and bomb a machine gun which held up the advance, and then destroyed another gun. Frickleton was awarded the VC for this action. Three other Kiwis – Sergeant Penrose, Lance Sergeant Thomson and Rifleman Dunthorne – were also recommended for VCs for their part in the fighting in Messines but these were not given. The 4th Battalion favoured their own methods:

> *'Smoke bombs proved of utmost value at this stage and the enemy who had taken shelter in cellars were soon smoked out and either killed or taken prisoner'.*

Slowly and with mounting casualties the New Zealanders were taking control. One of the last strong-points to be subdued was a machine gun post working in the ruins of Messines church and nearby, in the strong concrete cellars of the Abbey, the Ortskommandant, or German commander of the Messines garrison, Captain Thomas and his staff, were found and taken prisoner. An officer of the Royal Australian Engineers, Major Carre Riddell, later found there a set of maps showing the positions of German artillery batteries and headquarters which supplemented existing intelligence. One machine gun near the village square was found to be firing from a medical dressing station, considered by the New Zealanders to be sacrilegious, so Private White, the Company barber, who had already cleared an enemy dug-out and killed a sniper, led a party against it and killed the crew, an act for which he was awarded the DCM.

On the northern outskirts of the village were a number of concrete machine gun emplacements which had to be dealt with. Machine guns by the main Wytschaete road at Swaynes Farm, where the New Zealand boundary joined the British 25th Division on its left, held the attack up for a while until a tank crashed through the wall and subdued the post, forcing the machine gunners to surrender. Eventually the fighting was out on the eastern edge of the village and the day's objective, the trenches on the far side, with the views over the eastern slopes, were being reached. A strongpoint on the northeast boundary, a mill named Blauwen Molen, a fortified artillery headquarters, was to be overcome and a detachment of the 1st Wellington, under 2nd Lieutenant Blennerhassett, was sent to deal with it. A short sharp fight took place in the trench around the mill before the German commander and his men, a total of 27 prisoners, gave themselves up; elsewhere along the trenches the fighting was dying down. The strongpoint of Blauwen Molen was then to become a Regimental Aid Post. The 1st Auckland Battalion, who had marched around the southern edge of the village to avoid the shelling, moved forward to take the final part of the

AEROPLANE of 42ND SQUADRON R.F.C.
II ANZAC

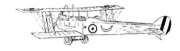

AEROPLANE of 53RD SQUADRON R.F.C.
IX CORPS

N.B. CONTACT AEROPLANES CARRY TWO BLACK
STREAMERS ATTACHED TO RIGHT HAND LOWER PLANE

Coloured identification drawings of contact aeroplanes were issued to infantry commanders; when certain positions were taken signals, normally using green flares, were given to spotters in the plane.

morning's objectives, Unbearable Trench. This they accomplished with little difficulty, they were also pleased to add two field guns to their trophies. It had taken almost $2\frac{1}{2}$ hours, as scheduled, to capture the trenches on the eastern crest and the New Zealanders began to dig in and consolidate their new positions. The commanding officer of the 1st New Zealand Brigade, Brigadier-General C Brown, came up to the village to oversee the works but was killed by a shell near the Moulin de l'Hospice.

As the German defensive principles were known to be founded on a swift counter-attack the New Zealanders, like the Australians to the south of them, brought up machine guns and artillery to pre-determined positions and awaited the onslaught. This came shortly after noon, later than they expected (a tactical error had resulted in the Eingreif, or counter-attack, troops of the 1st Guard Reserve Division being too far back) and those Germans who got through the British artillery barrage came up against the New Zealand machine guns, few managed to get beyond their Sehnen or Oosttaverne Line and the attempt petered out with considerable German losses. The water supply in Messines village was tested and reported to be poisoned, containing three per cent arsenic, although this was later found to be incorrect and the water was passed as being fit to drink.

The 25th Division had 800 metres, several German trench lines and the Steenbeck stream to cross before they came up level with the New Zealanders on their right flank as the German lines jutted out towards Spanbroekmolen. The German front line contained two strongpoints in farms; Ontario Farm was the site of one of the mines and this went up at 3.10 with the others and obliterated the position. The other, Mortar Farm, was dealt with by heavy artillery and neither posed any threat to

Peckham crater today. Behind the crater the ground falls gently to the Steenbeek before climbing up to Wytschaete on the hill top beyond.

the infantry. The first waves of troops went over as the Ontario Farm debris subsided, the 2nd Royal Irish Rifles plodding past the steaming marsh where the fortified farm buildings had been, to work their way along the remains of the front line which here ran east-west. The 13th Cheshires by-passed the remains of Mortar Farm, where they had lost Second Lieutenant Malone during a trench raid in May. Immediately behind them the 11th Lancashire Fusiliers found the front trenches to be in very poor condition after the week of shelling and the Steenbeck stream almost non-existent, except for wet shell holes. All battalions found the ground to be difficult to cross as the climb up the hill became fairly steep, but opposition from the Germans was weak as isolated groups readily surrendered and "the few who refused were quickly disposed of with the bayonet". Machine guns at Hell Farm were subdued and it was only as the troops reached the Messines-Wytschaete road that resistance was encountered. Middle Farm was found to be giving trouble to the 9th Loyal North Lancashires so Captain T. Thompson with B Company of the 2nd Royal Irish Rifles

The bunker to be found on the outer edge of the rim of Spanbroekmolen crater in which were found four dead German officers, with no apparent wounds or marks. They had been killed by the concussion of the mine explosion. No. 35 on map, page 135.

worked round the right flank to the back and took the strongpoint and four machine guns. Captain Thompson was killed soon after this exploit.

Having fought their way over nine trench lines the 25th Division were digging-in on the far side of the crest - the day's objective - after one hour and 40 minutes. Forward Observation Officers of the artillery set up artillery observation posts on the east side of the road, but the view proved disappointing owing to trees and hedges.

The Ulstermen of the 36th Division had in front of them one of the strongest sectors of the German front line, the knoll of Spanbroekmolen, with fortified points, Kruisstraat and Peckham, which had caused the Princess Patricia's Canadian Light Infantry trouble the year before, on each flank. The tunnellers had prepared a concentration of mines because of this but had had problems with the Germans counter-mining and setting off camouflets, small subterranean explosions to destroy the workings. One of the mines at Kruisstraat had been flooded by a camouflet, requiring rapid re-tunnelling whilst the Spanbroekmolen mine had also been damaged and the firing charges replaced, but the Royal Engineers were not certain that it would work. Spanbroekmolen did indeed work, although it went up fifteen seconds late and, as the Ulstermen had by then left their trenches and started forward across No Man's Land, many were thrown off their feet by the force and a number were hit by falling stones and clay. Some of the victims of this fall-out are buried almost on the spot where they fell, in Lone Tree Cemetery at Spanbroekmolen. The concussion had some other strange effects, as after the battle quietened down many bunkers were found that contained German dead. One on the edge of the Spanbroekmolen crater was found to contain four dead officers with no apparent marks. This bunker can still be found on the northern edge of the site (no.35 on map). With the number of mine craters here being five on a short front (one of those at Kruisstraat was a double, with two craters) the Ulstermen had some difficulty in keeping direction but found the German defences and defenders were completely shattered and so they pressed on to the next objectives. They met little opposition, the exception being machine gunners at a few farms, but these crews were bayoneted or shot and the advance continued up the hill to the crest and the Messines-Wytschaete road. One determined group of Germans in and around the bunker at Pick House put up a struggle and the 10th Irish Rifles were held up here until some of them, using a captured German machine gun and grenades, besieged the group. The Germans and their battalion commander eventually surrendered. Lumm Farm was part of the final objective on the right flank. This was a large concrete bunker with several chambers, strongly defended by resolute Germans. The 15th Irish Rifles, lead by Lieutenant Falkiner, stormed the strongpoint; fighting around the ruins of the farm and the bunker included a hand-to-hand tussle between Lieutenant Falkiner and the German commander and one of the chambers was cleared by Riflemen Cochrane and Aicken using grenades. Due to the cluster of bunkers around the farm and the conditions which made precise identification of sites difficult the 25th Division also claimed the capture of Lumm Farm: Major Ogilvie and troops of the 1st Wiltshires killed or took prisoner the garrison of 40 Germans from a bunker at Lumm Farm, but as to which was the centre of the point of resistance neither Ulster or English battalion records agree.

During this time the northern, or left flank, troops of the 36th Division, the 9th and 10th Inniskillings, were working their way through the remains of the southern half of Wytschaete village with the 1st Munsters from the South on their left. The stronghold of Wytschaete was no more: they went through the rubble of the village without difficulty, the one point of opposition, a machine gun, was put down by a tank called on by a sergeant of the 9th Inniskillings. Like the divisions to the right the Ulsters were on time and began to consolidate their gains.

The 16th Division, comprised of battalions from southern Irish counties, had as their boundaries the roads from Wytschaete to Kemmel, which was marked on trench maps as Suicide Road, and the road to Vierstraat. The mine under the German strongpoint at Maedelstede Farm, on a slight promontory overlooking the Irish, and the two at Petit Bois, were blown to minimise any opposition.

The pill box in Wytschaete Wood that held up the Irish advance until the machine gun crew were killed. No. 19 on map, page 135.

Maedelstede Farm was wholly successful in eliminating the German defences, as were the two at Petit Bois, but these were twelve seconds late and caused some casualties to the first Irishmen over the top.

One of the first to fall, near Maedelstede Farm, was the Irish Nationalist MP, Major William ('Willie') Redmond, of the 6th Royal Irish, who had been told he was too old, at 56, to join the attackers but had been allowed to after he had begged the division's commanding officer, Major General Hickie. Redmond was wounded in the hand but continued forward until hit again in the leg and, being unable to stand, was carried back. The stretcher-bearers who collected the Nationalist MP from the battlefield were Ulstermen from the 36th Division, he was taken to an Ulster first aid post and treated but unfortunately died of his wounds before being sent further back. Another senior officer of the same battalion was killed soon after as the 6th Royal Irish swept through the charred remains of Wytschaete Wood (almost a thousand incendiary drums had been hurled into the wood by the British three days earlier, in addition to the very heavy shelling). Germans in a

The ruins of Wytschaete after it was captured by the two Irish divisions on 7 June. IWM Q5460

concrete bunker with a machine gun in the wood caused a hold up and were rushed, when Captain O'Brien-Butler was shot. The remains of the bunker, no. 19 on map, can still be found in the wood, behind the British cemetery.

Petit Bois, which up till now had been impregnable, was taken without any difficulty as the German defenders of the 4th Grenadier Guards and 33rd Fusiliers were completely demoralised by the two mines. The 7th Leinsters, together with the 7th/8th Irish Fusiliers, encountered pockets of resistance as they took more trenches and dealt with these with little loss. A stubborn defence was met at a strongpoint in the buildings of l'Hospice on the northern edge of Wytschaete and this was surrounded and by-passed to be dealt with later. The Irish established a dressing-station at l'Hospice and their chaplain, Father William Fitzmaurice, tended the wounded while wounded himself, for this he was later awarded the MC. The site of the Hospice is today the village sports hall and playing field. Germans holding out at Red Chateau and the small wood between Wytschaete Wood and Grand Bois, named Unnamed Wood, also did not want to move until forced to. After the battle Unnamed Wood became officially named

Modern view of the ground in front of Hollandscheschuur taken from the site of the British front line. The Loyal North Lancashires and the Cheshires crossed this to find the mines had completely obliterated the Germans and their defences.

Inniskilling Wood at the suggestion of Major-General Hickie, who gave directions for a board bearing this name to be erected there. Unfortunately this name change was not adopted by others and the wood was still Unnamed on later trench maps.

The Irishmen mopped up the remains of Wytshaete and passed through, to establish their posts in line with the other divisions.

The 19th Division, with battalions from the north and west of England and Wales,had the fortified adjoining farms of Plateau and Hollandscheschuur, surrounded by a trench called Nag's Nose, as an important obstacle to contend with and because of its dominating position three mines were exploded at the start of the battle. Behind the position was Grand Bois, a wood full of German trenches with command centres and strongpoints. On the north or left flank of the division was Croonart Wood, which was also known to be heavily defended.

The attacking troops of the division had been given a hot meal the previous evening as they set off for their assembly trenches and forty minutes before the mines went off at 3.10am they were issued with a tot of rum for fortification.

When the three mines at Hollandscheschuur went up in a triple gigantic explosion which rent the air the 7th Loyal North Lancashires and 9th Cheshires set off over No Man's Land to the German trenches, to find these hardly existed and the few Germans that were still there readily surrendered. Those that showed any sign of opposition were shot or bayoneted. The Cheshires passed through the remains of Grand Bois, which like Wytschaete Wood had previously been given a bombardment of about 1,000 incendiary drums as well as gas and high

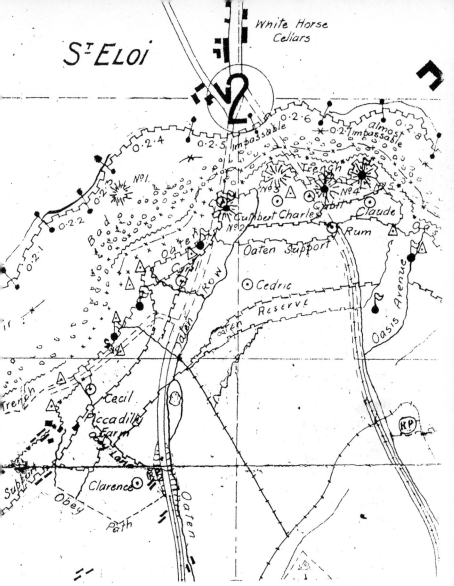

The map of the German trenches at St. Eloi which were the target of the battalions of the 41st Division. The mine crater was to be exploded under existing 1916 crater no. 3, and the front line, Oaten Trench. The mud and craters were expected to be more troublesome than the German defenders and the conditions in No Man's Land are marked as varying from 'Fair' to 'Almost Impassable'. The clusters of trench mortars (marked by a circle), which had given many problems, are marked and named – Cedric, Claude, Cuthbert, etc. Troops had been detailed to deal with any surviving the mine explosion.

explosive shells. They reported what was a similar situation elsewhere along the front:

> 'No opposition met with, a good many Germans were killed or wounded with the bayonet, and many more sent back as prisoner'.

Infantry went through Croonart Wood to find it almost empty and the bunkers there abandoned. The Cheshires and other battalions of the division had tunnellers from the Royal Engineers attached to them to reconnoitre the captured dugouts and bunkers in the woods. As soon as the go-ahead was given the battalion headquarters moved forward to the strongly fortified buildings on the edge of the wood at Onraet Farm, where they found stores of concertina wire and other stores which they then used to consolidate their position as arranged.

The 8th Gloucestershires and 8th North Staffordshires passed through to take further trenches towards the Black Line, the day's objective, but found the going so easy they kept going to Oosttaverne Wood, where more Germans either rushed forward to surrender or retired, none putting up any fight. Outposts were then established in front of the new British line and consolidated against counter-attack.

The German soldiers in the salient at St. Eloi, which had changed hands several times during 1915 and 1916 and had been an area of intense mining activity, suffered the largest mine explosion of the day. The mine, under craters 2 and 3 where The Mound had been before the March 1916 offensive, contained the largest amount of explosive, 95,600 lbs of Ammonal, but because of the warren of earlier workings the tunnel, at a depth of 38 metres, was by far deeper than the others. The Royal Engineers were disappointed with the results of the St. Eloi mine, later reporting that because of the extra depth in the stiff clay, which was very tenacious and resistant to disruption, the mine crater was not as large as hoped for. However the infantry of the 41st Division certainly noticed it because it woke them from their dreams. The 21st (Yeoman Rifles) King's Royal Rifle Corps had had a long march to reach the British trenches opposite the craters, and recorded:

> 'The men of the battalion, true to the natural characteristics of the British soldier, went to sleep when waiting for Zero. The explosion of the mine, however, under the St. Eloi craters woke them up and the whole battalion, in the formation under which they had been trained, advanced to the assault'.

The officers who watched it go up and remove the German front line and the strongpoint there, were delighted with the result. The 21st King's and the 32nd (East Ham) Royal Fusiliers passed the smoking crater as the giant lumps of clay were still settling down, to find the remaining Germans in the area not in any condition to oppose them. The front and support lines, which included the fortified 1916 craters, were practically unrecognisable and the troops pressed on to their next objectives. The Yeomen and men from East Ham found Germans eager to give themselves up although a few needed persuading with grenades to leave their dugouts. One German officer was seen to shoot himself in a dugout, which was an unusual occurrence.

The 26th (Bankers) Royal Fusiliers, passing through the 32nd, were especially keen to go over the top. They had left Aldershot fourteen months earlier, and had been initiated into trench warfare at Ploegsteert Wood, being based at The Piggeries. They had taken over the St. Eloi trenches towards the end of 1916:

> *'After 6 long weary months of waiting in the St. Eloi sector, overlooked by the enemy, every movement and every turn observed, all ranks were assembled with one thought – to get the Boche out of it'.*

Their objective was the private access road which ran in a straight line from the St. Eloi-Oosttaverne road to the White Chateau. They had been told it was 'strongly fortified and supposed to be a bit of a stumbling block'. They found that the artillery had prepared the Germans well for them; as the barrage lifted the Bankers rushed in and captured the position with very little resistance and before large

The bandsmen of the Bankers Battalion, who were to act as stretcher-bearers during the battle, just before they left England for the trenches on the Franco-Belgian border. The number of wounded on 7 June was not high for a WW1 battle (5 officers and 161 men, many of whom were 'walking wounded') but with the numbers of German casualties and the condition of the ground they were to have a hard day's work.

BAND OF THE 26ᵗʰ BATT (BANKERS) R.F.

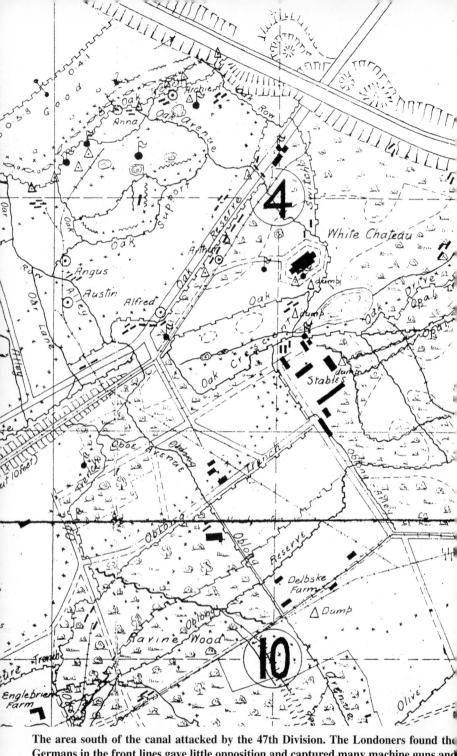

The area south of the canal attacked by the 47th Division. The Londoners found the Germans in the front lines gave little opposition and captured many machine guns and the trench mortars named Anna, Angus, Alfred etc. Things changed when they reached the White Chateau, where the defenders put up a strong resistance in the rubble.

The pile of rubble that was the White Chateau, home of the Mahieu family. The Germans had made a veritable fortress in the ruins, with shell proof safety in the cellars, and the Londoners had some difficulty in extricating them. The position was then used as a battalion headquarters by the British, and the Australians later built an observation post in the heap of rubble. No. 25 on map, page 135.

numbers of the Germans, who had been sheltering in strong concrete dugouts, were able to come out and fight. The prisoners were not counted before being sent back to the British lines but were estimated at between 300 and 400. There was one exception to the almost total surrender – as elsewhere along the line, an isolated machine gun crew put up some resistance before being knocked out.

The 124th Machine Gun Company and Royal Engineers moved up to join the Fusiliers in establishing forward positions and strongpoints: on time, and with minimal casualties, the 41st Division had established itself on the line of its final objective for the day.

Londoners of the 47th Division had the German lines astride Comines Canal to deal with, on their left was the 23rd Division, who although it was taking part in the Battle of Messines, were actually off the ridge, tackling the Germans at Hill 60 and The Caterpillar, where mines were to go up. The 47th Division did not have any mines on its section of front but the artillery barrage was as heavy as elsewhere. The Londoners south of the canal, the 6th, 7th and 8th Battalions London Regiment, took the first German lines and overcame the limited opposition without difficulty, but as they approached the rubble of the White Chateau trouble began. The defenders had made a strong fort out of the ruins and the attack was held up by Germans in the strongpoint with machine guns and showers of stick grenades. The position was strong, five metres of fallen masonry, beneath which

A pause after the battle. Marten's Farm, near the top of the Dammstrasse, had been a German strongpoint but was captured without difficulty.

concreted cellars concealed a number of snipers and machine guns. The Londoners tried to storm the position but failed, so they tried again but to no avail. Trench mortars were brought up and used to bombard the Germans inside, after which a third attempt, which this time proved successful, was made. The Germans were stubborn but the Londoners were determined and scrabbled over and through the ruins under intense machine gun fire. At one point Sergeant Major Bitton of the 6th Londons climbed on to the top of the heap of rubble and threw grenades at two machine gun crews on the far side; when he ran out of grenades he threw bricks and waved for two officers, Captain Ordish and Major Maynard, to advance round the side. The 7th Londons were also in the fray and threw smoke bombs down the entrance to the cellars below the ruins, the surviving Germans who emerged, an officer and 63 troops, were made prisoner. The Londoners were then able to make progress through the land around the chateau that had once been a green and pleasant park, and continue to the objective. The Royal Engineers of 520 Field Company came forward to convert the German strongpoint into a British one, (working as 'a tank was burning merrily at the White Chateau') and named it 'Mildren S.P.' after one of the commanding officers of the infantry brigade which had taken it. The 11th Royal West Kents, when they relieved the Londoners, established their battalion headquarters in the former German shelter of the chateau cellars, and found themselves reasonably safe from German shell fire with the thickness of cover above them.

Chapter Six

1917. THE BATTLE CONTINUES

By the end of the morning Plumer and his staff were pleased by the fact that all the planning and arranging had worked and the objectives had been achieved on time, and with relatively few casualties. Two hours after the start and the mine explosions the German trenches on the near side of the ridge were in British possession. A few hours later, after fresh troops had leap-frogged the first waves, the trenches on the far side of the crest were also taken and consolidated, and a German counter-attack had been beaten off. It was at the consolidation stage that most of the British casualties were to occur: because losses were much lower than had been allowed for the crest of the ridge and forward positions were crowded, and as the troops were digging-in they were in full view of the German machine gunners in and behind the Oosttaverne line. The Germans made full use of what they saw as a tactical error. Plumer decided that it was now time for the last and main objective of the day, the Oosttaverne Line or Sehnenstellung, to be captured. The afternoon attack was to commence at 3.10 pm, precisely twelve hours after the first.

The front had now become much smaller in length and a lesser number of troops were to take part. The 4th Australian Division, rugged and battle hardened troops who had recently had a hard time at Bullecourt, were to take the south end of the line, the 11th Division a length of the centre, and the 24th Division the northern end. Artillery moved forward to pre-arranged positions where ammunition had been stockpiled and began a systematic bombardment of the German defences and gun batteries behind the line. Twenty four new tanks were brought up to augment those which had already arrived from the morning contingent (many had not made the fighting as they were unable to cross the cratered areas and clayey mud from the initial shelling).

The attacking troops did not all assemble at the same time; the Australians were ready and in position for several hours, during which time they had to lie down under German shell fire and incurred many casualties before the 11th Division arrived. These were late because the orders to move forward were delayed and as the troops had marched during the night and were then rushed forward from Kemmel. In a forced march in the hot sun they were not in the best condition to attack, and because of this battalions of the 19th Division, who were closer to the front, were ordered to assist.

The Germans had spent the morning trying to assess their changed situation; the commanders were not aware of the British plans but presumed that an attempt on the Oosttaverne Line was likely and brought up available reserves. Elements of the 1st Guard Reserve Regiment, who had tried to counter-attack but met the British attack, also joined the defenders.

The 4th Australian Division came up against concerted machine gun and rifle fire from the Oosttaverne line, and field guns at Delporte Farm, and many were killed or wounded. The defence line consisted of many concrete pill boxes inside which the Germans had sheltered from the British barrage, emerging as the Australians approached. This was the Australian's first experience of bunker fighting. The Queens-landers of the 47th Battalion had to contend with two pill boxes astride the Messines-Comines road (then called Huns' Walk, nowadays the N314) and these were both scenes of bitter and bloody struggle but after acts of individual bravery the 47th ended up in control of them. Machine gunners in a pill box in the first trench of the Oosttaverne line where it crossed the Messines-Warneton road, 200 metres south of Huns Walk, fired on and killed men of the 37th (Victoria) Battalion and stopped any progress there. Captain R. Grieve, seeing that his men were pinned down by the machine gunners and continuing to become casualties, and a trench mortar and machine gun which should have

German pill box on the Oosttaverne Line where it crossed 'Huns' Walk', the road from Messines to Comines, the N314. This was attacked and taken by the 47th Australian Battalion; the picture was taken several months later, and grass now covers the ground. The site is now a house.

been available were put out of action by German fire, decided to take matters in hand. Rushing from shell hole to shell hole with a bag of grenades he reached the pill box and rolled two grenades through the gun aperture then ran round the back, to find the crew dead or dying. This allowed the men of the 37th to occupy the trench, but Grieve was soon wounded by a German sniper whilst signalling to some of his men. He was awarded the VC for his bravery in removing the threat to his men and enabling the attack to continue. Once the Germans in this stretch of the Oosttaverne line saw that the Australians

R.Grieve, VC

were breaking through they panicked and either surrendered or fled. This section of the front trench of the defence system now being in Australian hands, the next task was the support trench which also contained pill boxes and stubborn German machine gunners and the Australians had to quell them.

To the north of Huns' Walk, the Warneton road, the Oosttaverne Line followed the land which dips down into the wide and shallow Blauwepoortbeek valley and the Germans had sited many guns here; most of it was out of site of the observers on the crest of the ridge. The Australians attacked the line and made some progress, capturing most of the first trench, but then came under withering machine gun and artillery fire. The battalions were divided as men gained whatever shelter they could. Captain Young of the 45th Battalion, although already wounded, lead his men on towards the cause of the hold up, a group of concrete blockhouses from where German field guns were firing. He was killed in the attempt and the 45th could get no further forward. To the north of the Australians the British troops of the 11th Division had still not arrived and so the Australians, to cover their own flank, took some of the Oosttaverne line, as far as Polka Estaminet which they later handed over to the Border Regiment as a front line post, the concrete blockhouse of which can still be found by the St. Eloi road, the N336.

The 24th Division, tackling the northern stretch of the Oosttaverne Line, had an easier time of it, taking many pill boxes, some artillery, and numerous prisoners. Hence the full stretch of the afternoon's objective, the Oosttaverne Line, was in British hands except for the stretch in the Blauwepoortbeek valley. Later in the afternoon the Australians in the forwardmost positions saw Germans behind the line manoeuvering for a counter-attack, and signalled to the rear for an artillery barrage to halt it. The barrage came but whilst falling on the Germans it fell on the Australians as well. As they were being shelled

The last surviving remnant of the group of concrete bunkers which caused the 45th Australians so much trouble during the second stage of the attack, this one held artillery which fired at close range. In attacking this Captain Young and other Australians were killed. The bunker, which is a very strong construction, today houses cattle. After it's capture the immediate area was named 'The Better 'Ole'. No. 32 on map, page 135.

and having to fight off the Germans, some fell back towards the line gained in the morning, which was by now fully consolidated. This lead to other parts of the line being vacated as rumour of a retreat spread as senior officers tried to prevent men from falling back, sometimes leaving the wounded behind.

The commanders on the ridge ordered a protective artillery barrage where the Germans were thought to be, but with the confused situation this fell onto the Australians still holding out. The 45th Battalion, who suffered many losses from this artillery from their own side, recorded:

> *'this was most unfortunate as it inflicted a number of casualties on our men. After 'sticking it' for another hour the two companies together with the 47th Battalion had to retire'.*

Before long all of the southern length of the Oosttaverne Line, which had given the Australians so much trouble, and the gains opposite that stretch across Blauwepoortbeek, had been abandoned to the Germans. Fortunately the Germans did not realise this, as their own troops - who were newcomers and did not know the locations – were unsure of which trenches they held themselves. They re-occupied some small stretches, thinking that their artillery had blown the British out. Hence during the night of 7 June, in the confusion, neither side knew what the situation was or where the front lay.

The Australian commanders instructed that the line vacated be re-taken but, owing to the confused situation and lack of information, not all of the battalions were ordered forward in time and only the section south of the Warneton road was re-taken at first; this was not difficult as the Germans had not taken advantage of the Australian's absence.

The situation remained uncertain for the next two days as the Australians repeatedly tried to capture the stretch of line across the Blauwepoortbeek valley. The 50th and 52nd battalions continued the pressure during the night of 10/11 June, with a bombing attack down the trenches in the valley, when they found some of the German trenches to be empty and saw some defenders leaving the support positions. The Germans had vacated the whole of the Oosttaverne Line and withdrawn eastwards to their next defence system, the Warneton Line or Nachhutenstellung. The Gruppe Wytschaete commander, General von Laffert, had intended at this stage to fall back even further to beyond the Comines canal but, on seeing that the British had stopped at the Oosttaverne Line, General Sixt von Armin decreed that the Warneton Line was to be held at all costs. He also sacked von Laffert for tactical errors in placing his two counter-attack divisions, on which the elastic defence system depended, too far to the rear to be in position when needed.

The German withdrawal of 11 June was effectively the end of the 1917 Battle of Messines. The British put out patrols to examine the vacant land beyond the Oosttaverne Line and establish a forward line of posts; finding that the observation to the east was not as good as had been expected Plumer decided to push forward the front line. This was to be completed on the 14th but in practice the line was already forward and the posts and trenches merely needed joining up. Delporte

The artillery bunker which still exists at Delporte Farm, this was the control post for the battery which held up the Australians and prevented them from moving down the Blauwepoortbeek valley. Eventually the Germans abandoned it when they retired to the Oosttaverne Line, the British front line was then just east of the adjacent road the N336. The bunker was built inside the farmhouse which stood here and the original brick walls were incorporated. No. 31 on map, page 135.

Farm, the site of the German artillery batteries which had caused the Australians so much trouble, was occupied by a patrol of the 11th Division and the Australian 50th Battalion, the British troops then went on to form the front line just east of Wambeke hamlet and Joye Farm.

Another forward adjustment to the line was made on 31 July, at the same time as the main Ypres offensive began. The New Zealanders and Australians took the line of German forward posts close up to the Warneton Line. The centre of the line, opposite Houthem, was taken forward to close the gap there, making No Man's Land much narrower there also, and to the north the 41st Division took the bend of the canal and worked its way down towards Hollebeke, the 10th Queen's Royal West Surreys capturing on its way the large German command centre (now in ruins) in the gap between between the canal and the railway. The 18th King's Royal Rifle Corps, trying to push the Germans out of Hollebeke, found the German defences and dugouts were largely

The area between Hollebeke and the canal bend which the 41st Division captured on 31 July 1917, the last day of the Messines fighting and the opening day of the main Ypres offensive. This aerial photograph, taken ten days before, shows the condition of the ground over which the troops were to attack. After the repeated shellings the ground is a featureless landscape of water-filled shell holes and mud.

The German blockhouse at position 'h' on the German map page 107, clearly showing how it was constructed behind an existing brick building for concealment.

untouched by the artillery bombardment and were strongly held. They also found the mud to be a problem as most rifles became clogged and useless and all four Lewis guns were out of action. They managed to fight their way through using grenades, later reporting the attack to be 'only partially successful'. The 11th Royal West Kents were also being held up by machine guns in the ruins of the village, so troops under Captain Lindsey were sent to press the line through the village. At 11am Captain Rooney sent a message back to his commanding officer saying that Hollebeke was now in British hands.

By the end of the battle Plumer had fulfilled all his plans and all objectives were taken, however after the initial sweeping success of the siege warfare methods the operation had become bogged down in the centre and was only salvaged by the German withdrawal. British casualties had been about 25,000 (more than half of them Australian and New Zealand), very similar to an estimate of 23,000 Germans, although the two sides different accounting methods and periods prevent direct comparisons. The Battle of Messines was seen as a great success by the British, as it raised morale and showed what British planners could achieve. The Germans also regarded it as a masterstroke but thought the numbers of troops and services engaged to be excessive, and could not understand why the gains were not exploited further.

The tragedy of the victory was that it only served to allow the Third Battles of Ypres – 'Passchendaele' – to take place. The Australian, New Zealand and British divisions which had taken part in the battle were

German map of the lines at the Wambeke and Blauwepoorte-beek valleys after the fighting died down. The British front line, named Oldham Trench by the British (the position was first reached by the 11th Manchesters) was discontinuous and had three communication trenches: Bob Street to the southern end, Dorset Street in the centre, and Manchester Street to the north of the Wambeke. This latter trench wound past Freudental (joyful), known as Joye Farm to the British. The Germans had had a trench railway station and sidings here. Polka Estaminet, on König Strasse just above the 8km marker, and Delporte Farm, by the

Blauwepoortbeek, were existing concrete bunkers which were shown but not named as they were now in British possession. The German trenches and bunkers are shown, as is the line of their forward posts. Hohenzollern/Admiral Scheer Strasse is nowadays named Kaleute Straat, and most of the bunkers and other defences have disappeared. Ruppertsbau, a concrete infantry command post near Houthem, still exists, as does the concrete machine gun post marked 'h' to the east of square 7442. The bunkers which can be found today are all circled for identification.

British information map showing the British front line before the Battle of Messines, the line on 12 June, after the German retirement from the Oosttaverne Line, and the final gains, the line pushed forward on 31 July to give better observation over the Germans.

systematically taken out of the front and given time to rest and refit before action elsewhere, many of them in the forthcoming Ypres offensive. Battalions of the 11th Division stayed in the front and support lines, with working parties of infantry assisting sappers in the digging and wiring of trenches and strongpoints, gun pits, command posts and aid centres.

Both sides kept up the shelling, although at a lesser rate than before. The 37th Division then took over most of the line and continued to boost the defences, By late July the Engineers of the division were constructing permanent observation posts and shell proof shelters of reinforced concrete. Many of the German trenches were re-dug so the firing step and parapets faced the right direction and bunkers and dugouts were repaired and refurbished, some salvage of equipment was carried out and burial parties tried to identify and bury the dead, although this was difficult. German artillery observers and machine gunners behind their lines kept a watchful eye open for working parties and troops who exposed themselves to fire. Only one vestige of the 37th Division's works still remains, the concrete shelter adjacent to Derry House Cemetery No. 2, on the eastern slope of the ridge.

Troops of other divisions came and went, the 2nd Royal Welch Fusiliers passed through Messines in October, to man the front line trenches where they set up headquarters in an old German pill box. They noted:

> 'The village is only foundations, brick rubble, and a few stark pill boxes....The dead of both were still where they fell. From their attitudes it was easy to reconstruct the fighting round the pill boxes. It had been a fierce affair at close quarters, mostly with bombs.'

One of today's reminders: farmers still make use of the screw pickets which were used to hold barbed wire. The stake is screwed into the ground, designed to enable the pickets to be placed and wired in silence during the night, as working parties were liable to be shot at when knocking earlier patterns in. Germans and British used identical models, many of them being made in Sweden and sold to both sides alike.

Tasmanians in the front line in the winter of 1917/18. IWM E (Aus) 1331

Chapter Seven

1918. RETREAT AND ADVANCE

Late in 1917 the Australians, who like others had suffered in the Passchendaele offensive, and had subsequently been completely re-organised, took over the whole of the Messines front. The numbers of men in all units was low as reinforcing them became a problem. Losses in 1916 and 1917 had been high and recruitment had dropped as the natural supply of enthusiastic volunteers dried. In Australia a national referendum was held on whether to introduce conscription. The question was, "Are you in favour of the proposal of the Commonwealth Government for reinforcing the Australian Imperial Forces overseas?". The Australian public voted against conscription and the troops in Flanders meanwhile were having their numbers made up with returned wounded and sick men.

The re-organisation had resulted in the formation of the Australian Corps, to which all five of the Australian divisions belonged. The New Zealand and British divisions that were attached to the two Anzac corps were deployed elsewhere. Many of the senior posts that had been held by British personnel were filled by Australians, and plans to form another, the 6th, division were dropped, with its constituent units scrapped.

When the Australian Corps took over the Messines front it was a relatively quiet sector. All of the five divisions took turn in manning the front and rear defences and mounting trench raids to maintain the supply of intelligence and identities of German units opposite. As it was expected that at some time in the future, probably the spring, the Germans would launch a major offensive, schemes and plans were drawn up to greatly increase the defences, which were now to follow the latest British defence concept, i.e. the German method of defence in depth, with three distinct zones, rather than the previous system of fixed and rigid lines. Troops and commanders were also trained in what was to them a novel method of warfare - defensive, rather than offensive, fighting methods. The Australian Engineers and infantry working parties set about creating the forward, battle and rear zones with observation posts, artillery and machine gun emplacements, accommodation and command posts, many in reinforced concrete and also using old German constructions where appropriate. The Messines ridge and the ground where all the fighting had taken place in June fell into the forward zone, with the battle zone beginning on the western slopes and back to where the original British lines were. The Australian Engineers were impressed with the nature and solidity of much of the former German defences and the amount of work which had obviously gone into them.

The forward defence system, mainly on the eastern slope, consisted of wire entanglements, strongpoints and machine gun posts, all overlooked by artillery observation posts that could direct fire. The wire entanglements were in in three bands. The first band, of 40-50 metres width was thinly strung out, to avoid distant observation, and filled in old trenches, ditches and drains to prevent infiltration along these. Belts of wire were also strung out at right angles to break up any enemy formation. The second and third bands were more dense, with barbed wire aprons 10-25 metres apart and set with gaps so as to channel attackers towards the machine guns.

Strongpoints consisted of independent fortifications, trenches with machine guns and fire steps for riflemen, set out with an all round field of fire, able to hold out in the event of being surrounded. Machine gun emplacements were generally for two guns, mainly Vickers, although some were specifically sited for Lewis guns, which had a shorter range

of fire. All accommodation and shelters were, where possible, to be able to withstand a hit from a 150mm shell, although many were still only classed as 'splinter proof'.

The Australian Engineers realised they had a major task in front of them, but were allocated fewer infantry working parties to assist them, as resting and re-training was specified by higher command. Over the winter of 1917/18, which was very cold and wet, drainage and maintenance of existing trenches became important. Heavy rains in October and November, followed by lower than normal temperatures and much freezing, created many problems.

Apart from the weather, the observant Germans also caused problems. They had constructed a strong and high concrete artillery observation tower in the church tower in the centre of Warneton, and this overlooked all the eastern and southern parts of the ridge and the rear areas and brought artillery shells down on what it saw. The 7th Australian Engineers recorded its effect:

'Warneton Tower, an exceedingly strong ferro-concrete structure, about 14 feet square and 60 feet high, in Warneton. This O.P. observed practically the whole area, with the exception of a few dead spots, and this hampered works in so much that a large proportion of the work that might otherwise have been done by daylight had to be done by night which is much less effective'.

The Australian artillery tried to knock out the tower, but to no avail. On Christmas Day 1917 No. 6 Siege Battery of the Royal Garrison Artillery, with four 6" howitzers, fired 16 heavy shells at the tower but made no impression. They tried

Australians concreting a pill box on Messines ridge in the winter of 1917/18. The site has been camouflaged and the troops are hand mixing concrete. The empty cement barrels were rarely returned as they were a source of a valuable commodity, firewood.

2/12/1917

Christmas Eve, 1917. Outside the bunker all is not still but these German officers have found a tree to decorate.

again a few times but could not see any effect, so on 20 January they fired 100 shells at the concrete tower, with combined air and ground observation to guide the gunners. Seven direct hits were confirmed but it was apparent the tower still stood and was still in use.

Then the Australians tried the 'super-heavy' approach. The heaviest British artillery piece, the 15 inch howitzer, of which the Anzac Corps had been allocated one (the Second Army only had a total of three), fired its massive shell at the tower on 7 March 1918. The British Royal Engineers who carried out the engineering works for the siege howitzer were very impressed, and recorded the event:

'our 15 inch howitzer hit Warneton Church Tower (concrete observation post) and completely destroyed it'.

The quality of work carried out by the Australians on the defences was very high. Standard specifications were produced and worked to; these gave instructions on design, construction and workmanship, aspects of handling and storing materials, erecting camouflage, and completing the works. Concrete constuctions were strong and dugouts well timbered and drained.

Trench raids or enterprises became rarer as troops were to be kept fresh and rested for the defensive battle, although the Germans kept up their own sallies into the Australian trenches.Although the Australians had spent so much time and effort on the defence scheme at Messines they were not there when the Germans struck in April 1918, but had been sent south to assist in the defence of Amiens.

The 19th Division manned the defences from the Douve River up to the front of Wytschaete, with the Scotsmen of the 9th Division, assisted by the South African Brigade, covering the northern sector. This meant that the line was only thinly held, moreover the battalions which comprised the divisions were all below normal strength, having lost

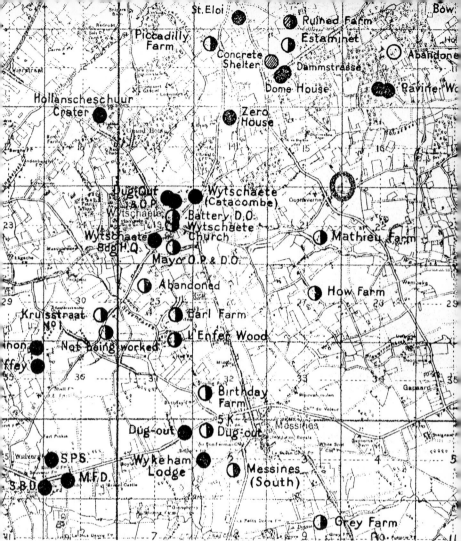

Some of the dugouts and concrete shelters being worked on by one Field Company in the early part of 1918. Of those marked on the map three can still be found: St. Eloi, Concrete Shelter and Messines (South). Other Field Companies also constructed shelters, often adapting earlier German ones.

men in the early days of the German spring offensive to the south. During the night of 9/10 April the Germans increased their shelling of specific parts of the British defences which, with observations of movements behind German lines, increased the tension as the British knew that an attack was likely – many had taken place further south – but it was not thought to be imminent. The early morning of 10 April

British bunker with two rooms at Scott Farm, on the road from Kruisstraat to Wytschaete, no. 18 on map, page 135. Constructed late in 1917, probably by the Australians, it was lost during the German offensive in April 1918.

was misty with poor visibility and the German Sturmtrupps, or storm troopers, of the 17th Reserve Division made good advantage of this, passing the front line posts and pushing back the 10th Royal Warwickshires and other battalions, getting as far as Messines village, where they took many Royal Engineers prisoner. The 8th North Staffordshires tried to recapture Messines, they made some gains on the outskirts but were unable to re–occupy the village. The front British line was then on the western slope of the ridge at Messines and then rose up the slope to cross the main road on the crest near Pick House. Wytschaete was still held and had not yet been attacked.

As the morning wore on the mist thinned out and visibility improved, allowing British artillery observers to direct fire onto the new German positions and this helped to stabilise the lines. The artillery had not fallen back when the Germans got close but volunteered to stay with the infantry, one 19th Division battery commander, Captain E.S. Dougall, was later singled out and awarded the VC for this exemplary behaviour.

E.S. Dougall, VC.

In the afternoon of 10 April the South Africans made a bid to clear the Germans from the crest near Pick House and Lumm Farm. After two and a half hours of fighting they were in possession of the remains of Messines centre and the eastern outskirts, but having incurred many losses they were unable to hold their gains and had to fall back to their original lines. The Germans were again in Messines, and were soon to continue the advance. They wanted Wytschaete, to have the observation it allowed over the British lines to the north, towards Ypres, an advantage they had had until June 1917. The troops which had held the village had been pulled out to stop gaps elsewhere, so a small patrol of the 5th Cameron Highlanders were sent to hold it from the Germans, this they managed to do until relieved during the night by the 12th/13th Northumberland Fusiliers and 2nd Lincolnshires who completely cleared the village of advanced German troops. In passing it is interesting to note that the 1st battalion of both these regiments had tried to wrest Wytschaete from the Germans when the war was still thought to be a mobile one, and the trenches a temporary expedient, in 1914. At dawn on 11 April, another misty morning, the line was therefore in front of the village, swinging round towards Oosttaverne Wood (Oosttaverne itself had fallen to the German 7th Division) and the Dammstrasse on the left. White Chateau was just in the British line, with the Germans in most of the parkland. British Generals were desperately scratching around trying to find reinforcements but as the Germans were making so much progress elsewhere this was difficult. The line at the Dammstrasse was thinly held by Scottish troops. The defenders saw figures emerging from out of the mist in the direction of Oosttaverne, and then took a heavy toll of the attacking Germans, who fell back realising they could not move forward. Further pressure caused the right of the line to swing backwards to Spanbroekmolen, so now the line here ran east–west, back towards Wulverghem and Neuve Eglise. After a few days, during which attack and defence battles raged at other parts of the front, the Germans massed for another concerted attempt to take Wytschaete, still held by assorted troops of the 9th Division, on 16 April. The Germans managed to work up the valley between Wytschaete and Spanbroekmolen, despite fierce opposition, and captured these two British strongholds. To the north of Wytschaete

The shelling continues. After Messines had changed hands several times little was left standing except for the concrete bunkers.

the British line was at Onraet Wood and was to hold here for another week. After that the whole of the ridge and the land to the west was back in German hands, although when things started to look less favourable to them, towards the end of August, they decided to give up some of their gains and fall back: from 6 September their front line was once again the Messines Ridge.

The British were by now in less of a defensive mood and were ready to harass and press the Germans, and began a series of small scale probes to test the defences. The 2nd Loyal North Lancashires sent Lieutenant Sharpe with some infantrymen to see if the mine crater in Petit Bois was strongly garrisoned during the night of 12 September. They found some of the trenches in the crater lip empty, but the Germans saw them and a fight ensued. The British retained control but could not move because the position was subjected to machine gun fire from behind the German lines. Ten days later they probed again, Second Lieutenant McKay and men left the trenches of the crater to examine the trenches in the wood itself; just inside the wood they met 15 Germans who opened fire with rifles and grenades and so had to retire. They had determined that the Germans did not plan any large withdrawal just yet and would need to be forced back.

Once again the British were to push the Germans off Messines Ridge, this time for good. A major offensive was planned for all along the front in Belgium, with the intention off clearing the whole of the high ground around Ypres. The offensive began in the early hours of 28 September; the southernmost part of the first phase was the top end of the ridge, and the 20th Middlesex started with the capture of White Chateau. The British had some difficulty in dislodging the defenders from the old craters at St. Eloi, but eventually the muddy place was taken.

The 5th King's Own Scottish Borderers, of the 34th Division, took German prisoners and their machine guns at Piccadilly Farm while other men of the battalion, under Captain Gilmour, pressed the Germans in the stronghold of Croonart Wood and forced them out, capturing the command bunkers in the wood. The Borderers passed through the wood to the main road but were then held up by a group of four machine guns around Dome House at the end of the Dammstrasse and at the site of Marten's Farm. Captain Gilmour sent back a message to Battalion H.Q. requesting artillery fire to remove the machine guns; unfortunately the message took an hour to arrive and there was another 45 minutes delay as arrangements were made. By this time the 5th Argyll and Sutherland Highlanders had stormed and taken the machine guns themselves and moved forward; the artillery barrage then fell on the positions just gained, causing seven casualties so, to prevent more, the troops had to withdraw from the new gains. When the shelling subsided the Borderers advanced against the Dammstrasse again, and, with the aid of artillery overcame the opposition in the strongpoints here. During this fighting Sergeant McGuffie distinguished himself and was then killed; he was posthumously awarded the VC. The battalion headquarters moved forward to the Dammstrasse and the troops were told they would be 'resting' here for two days and bivouacked in wet shell holes and long grass. There was no

L. McGuffie, VC

shelter at all apart from corrugated iron sheets and some waterproof sheets. Much rain fell: hot meals and rum were provided but even the battalion diary, normally extolling the spirits of the men, recorded that rain fell all day, 'and again the men had a bad time'.

Units of the 34th Division had also tried to enter Wytschaete but had difficulty in doing so because of the German defences. The 2nd Loyal North Lancs were to make their way from the north, they pushed their way through Petit Bois and Unnamed Wood, dealing with opposition found there. Wytschaete Wood was less easy, snipers hidden amongst the burnt and charred stumps were driven out but a 77mm field gun firing at short range held them up. The site of the first building, for some time only a heap of rubble, was The Hospice, this was reached after darkness had fallen, but was taken and consolidated. The Lancashiremen could get no further into the village, but movement east was easier, so they sent men in that direction and captured the German position and the British 1917 cemetery at Somer Farm. The 5th Argyll and Sutherland Highlanders had captured the ruins of Red Chateau and its defenders and were working their way through to the eastern edge of Grand Bois when they too came under fire from German positions on the northern edge of Wytschaete. They set up headquarters in the German bunker which is still in the middle of Grand Bois before clearing Onraet Farm and Wood and reaching the main road.

See Map page 120

The Germans had prevented the British from re-taking Wytschaete, but saw they were being encircled: during the dark they trickled out of the village, leaving the Lancashires to enter the village at first light on 29 September.

Meanwhile Germans were seen to be pulling out of Messines and down the eastern slope towards the Canal; a patrol of 2/15th Londons of the 30th Division entered the village but, as it was now dark and no

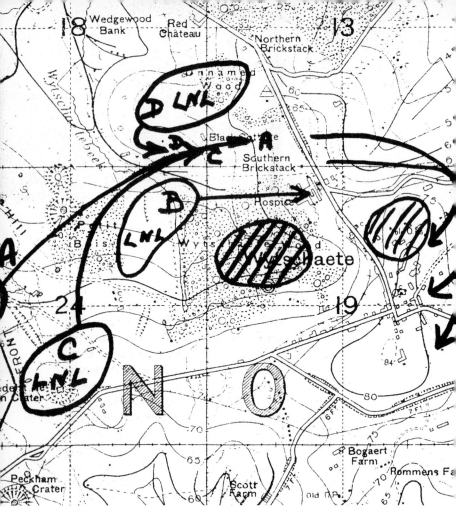

Map of the Loyal North Lancashires, illustrating how they encircled Wytschaete and entered from the east. The hatched areas are specific groups of German defenders.

streets or buildings existed for navigation, they decided to wait for morning before proceeding further and fell back to Moulin de l'Hospice for the night. The following morning saw Messines in British control, and so the Germans began to shell it. The 31st Division pressed its way up and over the southern slope, the ground won by the Australians in June 1917, to encircle Messines and the remnants of the garrison there. The Germans put up limited opposition at the double Ash Crater (formerly Trench 127 Left and Right), from the 1917 mine explosions. Then, using some of their 1917 concrete pill boxes and an old British communication trench named 'The Only Way', slowly

British concrete artillery headquarters bunker, dating from the winter of 1917/18, at Hiele Farm, no. 23 on map, page 135. It was built into the lee of the high ground behind, although it was damaged by being hit by a heavy shell.

withdrew whilst fighting rear–guard actions.

The 41st Division on the following morning pressed down on the rear of the ridge from the north, taking possession of Hollebeke and the Comines canal down as far as this village, as the 34th Division passed through Wytschaete and down to Oosttaverne, meeting almost no opposition on the way. The men of the two divisions then closed in on the canal and the defences there; the retreating Germans did not make use of what had in 1917 been the Warneton Line as the British were outflanking them from the north. The 23rd Middlesex had the job of clearing the area around the Comines Canal. The task initially was not difficult, their commanding officer reported that they moved in diamond formation, lead by Lieutenant Meester, and progress was good: 'advance exceedingly rapid, prisoners being taken freely, as opposition slight', but as they worked their way down the canal things began to get more difficult. They came under fire from machine guns along the canal near Houthem, one hold–up was removed by a group under Sergeant Potts crossing the canal and returning with 35 German prisoners and 3 machine guns. Other machine guns along the canal also prevented further movement forward and the Middlesex, by now running out of ammunition, had to fall back by 200 metres, where they joined the 10th Royal West Kents whose advance had also been stopped. A German plane flew over, observing for, and directing fire from, a battery, and soon shells began to fall among the troops. The commander reported that 'things began to look exceedingly bad' and sent carrier pigeons with pleas for small arms ammunition and artillery cover. S.O.S. rockets were fired into the air and before long the situation suddenly looked brighter: large numbers of British troops (from the 30th Division, although the Middlesex could not identify them) were observed coming from the direction of Messines and at the same time the artillery barrage opened on the German positions. The Middlesex were then able to move forward along the canal, by the end of the day they had taken substantial numbers of prisoners and guns, together with four field artillery pieces. The concrete machine gun posts, the ruins of which are still in the railway embankment, and the artillery observation posts there which could direct fire onto the attackers, were the last German defences, and these had had their last effect on the advancing troops.

Eventually the fighting passed away to the east, as the Germans, almost in disarray but formulating plans to make a stand at Menin and Geluwe, were pursued by the British. The staff of the Advanced Divisional H.Q. for the 34th Division moved into the old German headquarters bunker on the east side of the railway embankment near Hollebeke and from there directed the fighting around Menin, but eventually even they went east.

The fights for Messines Ridge, and the villages of Wytschaete and St. Eloi, were over, for the next six weeks the area was a transit camp and stores area, meanwhile the battlefield was cleared and the many dead buried.

This former German bunker, in the east face of the railway embankment near Hollebeke, no. 28 on map, page 135, probably an artillery command post, which had connecting tunnels beneath the embankment which can be identified but are now collapsed, was the Divisional Headquarters of the 34th Division for the first two weeks of October 1918 after the Germans were pushed back off the ridge and the fighting was further east, around Menin.

Chapter Eight

MESSINES RIDGE TODAY

The war left Messines Ridge and its three villages in a completely uninhabitable condition. In 1919 searches were made for the bodies of the fallen of both sides and the small cemeteries, often begun while the battle raged, expanded. In later years these were consolidated into the sixteen Commonwealth cemeteries on and around the ridge today. All of the German cemeteries which were here have been removed. The countryside was a devastated wasteland filled with the detritus of war and special labour battalions, some comprising German ex-prisoners of war awaiting repatriation, were formed to clear this up and salvage whatever metals and materials could be found, and to fill in trenches and shell holes.

The fields contained many strong concrete bunkers, some of which were used as temporary accommodation by returning civilians, and the Belgian government paid contractors to remove most of these. This was also a means of disposing of the many shells which were found; these were placed inside the bunkers with a small explosive charge and detonated. The broken concrete, together with the rubble from the villages, was also a valuable commodity as all the roads had to be re-constructed. In 1920 the re-building of the villages began, farmers

The centre of Messines shortly after the war ended. Only structures which had been strengthened, usually for observation, are left standing. Beneath the rubble are a number of cellars fortified by the Germans. The villages of Wytschaete and St. Eloi were in similar condition.

Meessen Gentstraat na de slag
Messines Rue de Gand après la bataille

The ruins of Wytschaete shortly after the war finished. The road has been repaired but the only two buildings standing are the pill boxes on the horizon.

began to get the land under control again, and the communities re-established themselves. Shortly after this came the 'Pilgrims': wives, mothers, girlfriends and families of the fallen, who came on tours and individually to find the graves and memorials of their loved ones. Also returning were the soldiers who fought here, some with families and some with regimental reunions and old comrades. Henry Williamson recalled visiting the area several times in the 1920's, and did not get on well with the local inhabitants; during one visit he had a fight with some young men who were rude to his wife in a café near Maedelstede Farm and had to flee.

The cemeteries in the area, as elsewhere, are quiet, peaceful places with the ambience of a well tended country graveyard, kept in immaculate condition by the gardeners of the Commonwealth War Graves Commission. The cemetery register often gives a brief history and some details of actions which resulted in its being, and visitors are requested to sign the visitors book.

Messines Ridge Cemetery, no. 1 on map, on Nieuwkerkstraat (the road to Neuve Eglise) is the largest in the area and was started after the war, many graves from other cemeteries which were later cleared have been concentrated here. There are a number of special memorials to men known or believed to be buried here, and to men from other cemeteries which were destroyed in the fighting. The Cross of Sacrifice is on the site of Moulin de l'Hospice, a German strongpoint, and the New Zealand Memorial to the Missing, by the entrance, is the site of one of the associated buildings.

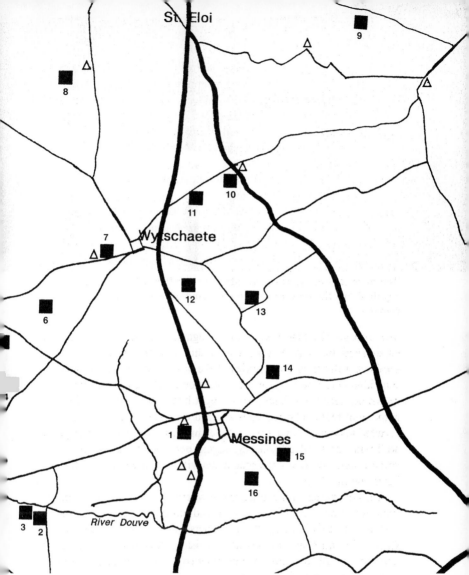

The cemeteries and memorials on Messines Ridge today. Some of the cemeteries, such as Messines Ridge and Oosttaverne Wood, contain burials from other graveyards which were later cleared and concentrated in these.

From the cemetery a good impression can be gained of the view over the British lines and rear areas and the ground the attackers had to cross before climbing the hill to the German lines. Also on the western edge of Messines is the New Zealand Memorial Park, located down Nieuwzeelandersstraat. This is dedicated to the soldiers from New

Zealand who fought in the June 1917 battle, it was unveiled by King Albert in 1924. A service of commemoration is held here by the New Zealand Ambassador each ANZAC Day, 25 April. By the edge of the park are two German concrete bunkers, on the site of Uhlan Trench, taken during the opening stages of the battle.

A new Peace Memorial, open in the autumn of 1998, has been sponsored by the Irish government to commemorate the joint action at Wytschaete of the 16th (Irish) and 36th (Ulster) Divisions on 7 June 1917. It is sited by the N365 to the south of Messines village, on the ground taken by the New Zealanders and possibly the only divisional or unit memorial on the Western Front to be some kilometres from the site of the deeds commemorated.

To the north of Messines village, by the Wytschaete road, is the Memorial to the London Scottish, for information on this see Chapter One.

La Plus Douve Farm Cemetery, no. 2, by the farm of that name, was used until the farm, known then as Ration Farm, fell to the Germans in April 1918. Headquarters and medical posts were based at the farm and the graves of many Canadians, buried when they held the line, are here as are those of several Germans, who received medical treatment as wounded prisoners. The track to the cemetery was named Plum Duff Street. Adjacent is the slightly smaller Ration Farm (La Plus Douve) Annexe, no. 3, also used until the British fell back in 1918.

R.E. Farm Cemetery, no. 4, was started next to the farm buildings during the early fighting, in December 1914, and consists mainly of burials from before the 1917 fighting. It is only just visible from the road and the entrance is easy to miss.

Spanbroekmolen Cemetery, no. 5, comprises almost wholly Ulstermen who fell on 7 June 1917, with the exception of one man from the 17th (Poplar and Stepney) Londons, who was some way from his division, the 47th. The cemetery is on the site of a German trench named Naples Switch and after the battle the British established a large rail siding, named Naples Siding, next to it. The view towards Wytschaete from the cemetery shows the ground the Ulstermen had to cross before reaching the main defence line around the village,

Spanbroekmolen crater, purchased after the war on behalf of Toc H in Poperinge to preserve it, is now known as the Pool of Peace. A memorial tablet at the entrance gives some details of the mine working and the crater dimensions.

Close by is Lone Tree Cemetery, no. 6, on the southern side of the hill. This was formed just in front of the British front line trench to bury the first Ulster casualties of 7 June 1917, many of whom were hit by fall-out from the mine explosion. In the spring of 1918 this trench was one of the major support lines against the expected German offensive, it was then named Ulster Road.

Wytschaete Cemetery, no. 7, contains graves of men from some of the first fighting in the area when the lines were being established in 1914 to when the village was finally liberated, in September 1918. Casualties from most of the intermediate battles are here also. A main German communication trench, Nab Street, ran through the adjacent field and the route of this can still be discerned as a slight hollow when the grass is at the right height. Next to the cemetery is the Memorial to the 16th (Irish) Division and all Irishmen who fell in the war. This is in the form of a Celtic cross with the Gaelic inscription:

> Do cum Gloire De
> Agus
> Onora na hEireann
>
> *(To the Glory of God and the*
> *Honour of Ireland)*

Croonaert Chapel Cemetery, no. 8, reached by taking the path across the field, is situated in what was No Man's Land before the 7 June 1917 attack. One of the burials here is a man of the Chinese Labour Corps, with the main inscription in Chinese and basic information – personal identification number (130) and date of death, probably killed whilst clearing the battlefield after the Armistice, in English. The

The 16th Division Memorial next to Wytschaete Cemetery.

other graves are mainly from 1917 with two later ones. There were some German graves but these were removed. The cemetery is named after a chapel which stood nearby on the German front line, the site of which can be found in a small copse in the trees by same side of the road, some large depressions in the copse are some small mines from 1915. The ruined chapel was the subject of an Adolf Hitler painting from when he was based in Croonart Wood. The small valley in which the cemetery sits was a trench railway siding named 'Purgatory' by the

British in the winter of 1917/18

By the side of the track which leads to Croonaert Chapel Cemetery is a small French memorial stone commemorating Lieutenant Lasnier and those of the French 1st Battalion Foot Soldiers who died here in the 1914 fighting.

Oak Dump Cemetery, no. 9 and the northernmost on the map, was started in the British support trench system. The 'Dump' was probably an Engineers or ammunition store, many of the trenches, British and German, in the vicinity were named Oak - Oak Trench, Oak Support, Oak Lane, etc, after the nearby Eikhof (Oakhouse) Farm.

Near the entrance to this farm, on the St. Eloi-Hollebeke road, is a small chapel, Eiken Hof, which contains a memorial to Second Lieutenant William Gordon Penrice, 20th Durham Light Infantry, who was killed close by on 17th June 1917.

The chapel at Eikhof Farm which contains the memorial to Second Lieutenant Penrice, and two French memorials.

At this period the 20th D.L.I. held the ground captured by the Londoners on 7 June, and Second Lieutenant Upton was also killed. The chapel also contains two French memorials to soldiers who fought and died around here during the early days of the war. A small private memorial stone is found by the farm on the corner as the site of White Chateau is approached. This is to two brothers who lived at the chateau, Auguste and Michel Mahieu, and were killed during the war.

Oosttaverne Wood Cemetery (no. 10), on the N336, was originally two separate cemeteries which were started immediately after the British attack. The wood, was in the fields behind the cemetery and the vestige of the wood, a small copse, can be seen about 200 metres to the west. The cemeteries were conjoined when graves were later brought here from other locations. Up the centre of the present site was a major German trench, Obstacle Trench, and it was probably in this trench that

Oosttaverne Wood cemetery. In the field behind the cemetery are two German concrete bunkers; these were later used by the British. Inset is the closest one to the cemetery.

the aid post which started the burial ground was based, as ground level would have been in full view of the Germans who were just to the east, over the road. In addition to the more than 1,000 British and Commonwealth dead an unknown number of Germans are buried here.

In the fields behind the cemetery, in what was once the wood, are two German concrete bunkers which were captured on 7 June. They were used as shelter by various British units over the winter of 1917/18, and both show signs of severe damage, probably shell fire. Both were constructed for accommodation, evidenced by the chimneys, for a stove, cast into the concrete rear walls.

Close to the entrance to the cemetery, at the crossroads, is the Memorial to the 19th (Western) Division, with its butterfly emblem, the battalions of which took this ground in 1917.

Somer Farm Cemetery, no. 11, was begun next to the ruins of the farm of this name which had been

The memorial to the men of the 19th Division near Oosttaverne.

Somer Farm after its capture by the British. The observation post and shelters inside have survived the shelling which destroyed the farmhouse and buildings. The strong concrete shelters were used by the British as battalion headquarters and the Australians later converted and repaired them. A field ambulance based here in June began the cemetery which was used until the Germans regained possession in April 1918. A few more burials were made in October 1918 when it was again in British hands.

converted into a strong concrete observation post and command centre by the Germans. The farm was subsequently used by field ambulances of the units which held the line and in January 1918 the 1st Army Troops Company, Australian Engineers repaired the concrete structure, which was by then badly damaged, and strengthened the east wall, facing the Germans. The bunker was destroyed after the war. The present-day farm is not on its original site.

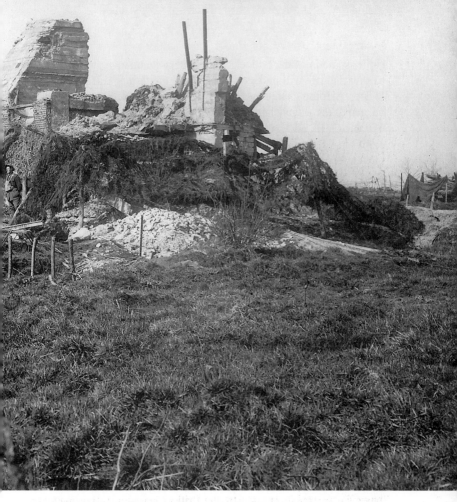

Torreken Farm Cemetery No.1 (no. 12 on map), the only one on this site, was started by the 5th Dorsets of the 11th Division who took over this sector and established an aid post in the German dugouts here. The dugouts have since collapsed but parts of the steelwork can plainly be seen sticking up through the ground close by. The entrance to the cemetery is through the garden of a house and across a field of

The remnants of one of the collapsed German dugouts that were used by the field ambulance which started Torreken Cemetery. The Australians also had an aid post and Battalion H.Q. here in January 1918. The 14 German burials in the cemetery were probably wounded prisoners.

cattle, sometimes the bullocks can be very inquisitive, and neglecting to shut the gate will understandably raise the farmer's wrath.

Derry House Cemetery No. 2 (there is not a No. 1), marked no, 13 on map, was established by a field ambulance of the 11th Division which was based in the farm ruins here in June 1917; some of the earlier burials are of the Duke of Wellington's Regiment that held and moved forward the line on 10 June. It was also used by the Royal Irish Rifles, who then named the farm. The road which gives access was named Antrim Road, and a number of Australians from the 47th Battalion were buried here in August of that year. This battalion took over Derry House and based their H.Q. here on 8 August, and had the 48th Battalion on their right and the 11th Royal Warwickshires on the left. They lost sixteen men whilst here, mainly by sporadic German shelling. Just before they were relieved and moved to Torreken Farm they recorded:

> 'August 21st. Completed cemetery at Derry House for all men of the battalion killed during operations in this sector, erecting crosses to all, perpetuating their memory. It is trusted that this cemetery may be preserved as a burying ground for men who gave their lives in the cause.'

The 37th Division held the line here for some time and the Royal Engineers of the division constructed a concrete command post for the field battery, the shelter is now built into the wall dividing the cemetery from the farm. On the other side of the wall the farm yard is paved with German concrete blocks, with the distinctive style of their pre-cast bunker system. The vantage point of the cemetery gives excellent views towards Hollebeke and the east: the British observers

The concrete command post in Derry House Cemetery constructed by 154 Field Company Royal Engineers between 13 and 25 July 1917 for a field artillery battery.

here had good observation across the Wambeke valley and over the Germans in the Oosttaverne and Warneton Lines. The farm was a strongpoint held by the 1st Wiltshires on 10 April 1918, although the morning mist obscured observation and the German stormtroops surrounded and by-passed it, then moved on to penetrate Messines village.

Cabin Hill Cemetery, no.14 on map, is on the edge of the ridge as it begins to slope down towards the east. The land on which the cemetery sits and the adjacent Fanny's Farm was one of the first main objectives of 7 June, they were taken by the New Zealanders after quelling some opposition here. It was begun by the 11th Division after they came up behind the first attacking troops to take the line of advance forward on 7 June.

Bethlehem (or Bethleem) Farm gives its name to two cemeteries, East (no. 15) and West (no. 16). Bethlehem Farm East, the smallest cemetery on the ridge, is the location of a German headquarters and strongpoint captured by the Australians whose field ambulance set up a field hospital here, and most of the burials are those who died in the first phases of the fighting. The Germans had established a headquarters in the farm in the winter of 1914/15 and Adolf Hitler, who was a messenger, was billetted here for a time. Hitler visited, the rebuilt farmhouse in the early 1940's, and presented the farmers wife with a bunch of flowers. The pillars at the entrance to the farm yard are constructed from stonework from the Abbey.

Bethlehem Farm West Cemetery is 250 metres away over the road and down the track. The farm here was named Schnitzel Farm and was one of the first gains when it was captured by the 38th Australian Battalion. Immediately outside the east wall of the cemetery was Ungodly Trench, one of the German defences which protected the

The cemetery at Bethlehem Farm East, site of a German stronghold captured by the Australians at the opening of the 1917 battle. All but one of the graves are of Australians.

strongpoint at Bethlehem Farm.

The majority of the craters resulting from the mine warfare on the ridge are still to be found, and can be visited although most are on private farm land and crops and stock should be respected. Factory Farm and Ultimo Craters, where the Australians attacked, are still there as is one at Trench 127 Right (Ash Crater), although the adjacent one has recently been filled and is now the site of a new factory unit.

Ontario Farm crater, next to the farmhouse, is small and sometimes barely discernible due to the nature of the ground. The ground rises slightly in front of the farm, but it was the ground to the south that it controlled and the Germans were able to prevent a direct assault on Messines village from here. Although the mine was effective in removing the strongpoint only a small and shallow crater was made. The three craters at Kruisstraat are nowadays fishing lakes where locals find sport in the still depths.

Peckham is easy to find and visit but the field is usually full of cows or young bulls, care should be taken with the latter. Maedelstede Farm is also a fishery with the name of 'Oosthoeve' and some of the fishing is competitive, so disturbance can be unwelcome.

The two craters at Petit Bois are not easy of access and some walking is required, although from the craters the vantage points can be appreciated. The wood itself is now fenced off and entry not normally permitted. If entry is gained or one of the clearings seen

Pile of shells on the edge of Croonart Wood, 1997. Croonart Wood, through which the German front lines ran, was for many years and into the late 1980s a private museum but closed when the owner, André Becquart, died. The trenches and a deep mine shaft in the wood had been maintained and the museum held a good collection of articles relevant to the German occupation and the fighting. The museum has since fallen into decay and some of the trenches have collapsed but most can still be found. The wood is still private property and entry is not encouraged.

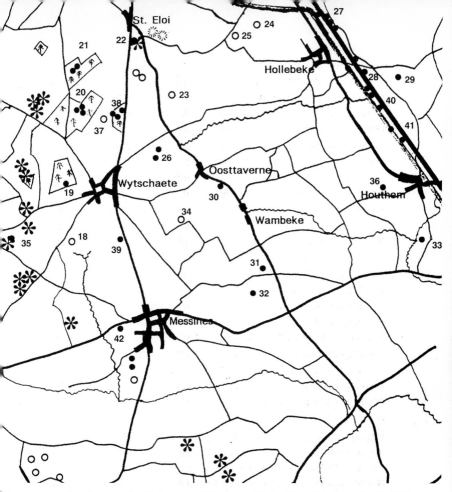

The concrete bunkers and pill boxes which can still be found today, the British ones (mainly built between July 1917 and February 1918) are marked with a circle, the German (all from before June 1917) with a solid circle. Many are in ruins and are little more than broken concrete with iron bars protruding, some are filled with water or earth, having been built at trench level, whilst some are still large constructions which can be entered. Most are on private land and this should be respected.

The majority of those built were demolished in the 1920's (concrete rubble was a valuable source of road base material) and some more are removed from time to time because of road improvements, housing and industrial development, or simply because the farmer on whose land they sit wants one removed. The development of bigger and more powerful construction machinery has made this easier than in previous years. In addition to those shown above a number of underground bunkers are known to exist in Messines and Wytschaete villages, beneath houses rebuilt after the war. The cellar of the BBL bank in Messines is believed to have been a particularly large and strong bunker, an ammunition store, but is obviously impossible to visit. Troops of both sides made use of the fortified shelters. When setting out their defence lines the Germans made good use of the existing cover of the railway embankment and built many command and administrative shelters here which were used during the Battle of Messines in 1917. Machine gun emplacements in front and artillery batteries behind were used in the 1917 fighting and also the final advance at the end of September 1918.

through the fence the rough and broken nature of the ground, old trenches and shell holes, will be seen. The farms at Hollandscheschuur were rebuilt close to their original sites after the war but the shapes of the three craters, and their dominant position over the British lines, can be seen.

The land around St. Eloi still retains much evidence of the mining activity there. The large number of smaller mine craters that were blown in 1915 have been filled for housing or ploughed, however the larger craters from the later activities still remain, filled with water. By the east side of the N336, and with access, will be found craters 4 and 5 blown on 27 March 1916 (see photo p.51). Behind the houses in the angle formed by the N336 and the N365 is a larger crater, that blown at the start of the main offensive on 7 June 1917, together with a smaller, earlier crater. Up until recently here, close to the N365, were the remains of a German pill box which was right on the front line and would have been constructed very close to the British, and must have been a success of planning and construction, however it was not much use when the mine went up. Near the large crater, and sited to fire across it, is a British standard pattern concrete pill box with machine gun embrasure, with the elephant iron internal casing still in very good condition, dating from the winter of 1917/18 when the Australian Engineers were very active here, no. 22 on map, page 135, see photo p.50. Further down the N336, just off on the left and close to the site of Hiele Farm, is a concrete bunker, probably a command post for the gun batteries based here in the spring of 1918. It was situated in the lee of the high ground behind, out of the sight of German gunners. It was probably constructed by the Australians, as was the small bunker whose ruin can be found in Oaten Wood and that of another just

The British bunker at Onraet Farm. This was home to battalions which held the line through the winter of 1917/18. Several German bunkers, which were also used by the British, are in the wood behind.

outside the copse. Oaten Wood, on the western slope of the slight ridge, was the terminus, named 'Porridge', of a rail system that brought up ammunition and supplies to the batteries around here.

The park which surrounded the White Chateau is now a golf course, with bunkers of a more peaceful nature. In the centre is the club house and close to this, in a small spinney, is the last of the heap of rubble that was the German stronghold and where later the 4th Field Company Australian Engineers constructed a concrete artillery observation post; this post can still be entered although golfers do not like visitors crossing the greens (no. 24). Next to the track running by the side of the course towards the canal is another concrete bunker, originally German but was adapted to provide shelter for the British, the blockwork wall built to provide protection from the Germans is still apparent, no. 25 on map, page 135.

Another concrete bunker, built

The end use of a German pill box and the recycling of materials. The farmyard adjacent to Derry House is paved with pre-cast concrete blocks, made behind the lines in Wervick, from a German construction pattern. The two holes in each block were to allow iron reinforcing bars to be threaded through to knit the blocks together. The resultant structure was very strong and would withstand a heavy shell. The concrete bunkers still in Croonart Wood are of this pattern, and these blocks can be seen at various sites around the Messines Ridge and the Ypres Salient.

by the British when the lines stabilised, is on the site of Onraet Farm. The large shell proof construction (no. 37) was built inside the ruined farm buildings (the farmhouse hearth and fireplace are plainly visible, cast into the concrete) which stood there by 153 Field Company, Royal Engineers of the 37th Division who commenced work on 9 August 1917. This was Brigade Headquarters and was used by the units in this sector, including the Australian battalions during the winter. Close by, just inside the edge of the wood, is the remains of the German headquarters which was refurbished and used for a while by the British. In the wood itself are three more German bunkers, in generally good condition although full of mud and water; one is in the centre of the wood and two are close to the main road (no. 38 on map).

Pick House, no. 39, by the side of the N365 just south of Wytschaete, is a small German bunker still in remarkably good condition as it changed hands several times. It was one of two which were here, originally well back from the road, which has been widened. When the 10th Irish Rifles reached the bunker at about 7am on 7 June the battalion commander and his staff inside did not want to surrender and resisted, so the Irish Rifles, protected by a German machine gun they found, threw grenades inside, forcing the garrison out to surrender. In April 1918 the Germans pushed the 10th Warwickshires, who were trying to hold the position, back in the direction of Wytschaete; the South Africans tried to regain the position and were partly successful but soon they too were forced to yield it to the Germans.

On the eastern side of the ridge a number of German shelters and bunkers, a small proportion of the many which were built, still remain. Along the N336 in the direction of Warneton will be passed the two bunkers at Oosttaverne Wood Cemetery, no. 26; Polka Estaminet, which was taken by the Australians and then held as a front line post by the British, now in the back yard of a rebuilt house, no. 30; Delporte Farm and the bunker at The Better 'Ole are described in earlier chapters. The German command post built into the former farm house (no. 33) and the Ruppertsbau (no. 36) bunkers near Houthem were both close behind the Warneton Line, which was the German front after the Battle of Messines, and both fell at the end of September 1918.

The line of the Comines Canal and the rail embankment behind it made a natural defence line and provided an ideal location for many shelters in dugouts and bunkers, most of these can be found today but many are in ruins following the artillery bombardments. At the northern end, between the railway line and the canal at Hollebeke, are the remains of what was a German headquarters, now in ruins (no. 27). This is found 100 metres from the underbridge, down the track into the overgrown area which is now a nature reserve. The bunker no. 28 was used as headquarters of the 34th Division early in November 1918, the tunnels through the rail embankment have now collapsed. There are ruins of others in the embankment, the machine gun position (no. 40 on map) the Germans called Juliusturm, now lacking its roof and without the tunnel through to the far side of the embankment, which held up the 23rd Middlesex and 11th Royal West Kents on 29 September 1918 until reinforcements arrived. The machine gun here, and others along this stretch, had prevented the British from getting past Hollebeke village after the Messines battle died down. Just south of this, at the site of the ruins of the old canal lock, Schleuse 4, can be found the German commander's bunker, no. 41 on map.

Towards Kortewilde, built into a farm unnamed by the British and called simply position 'K' by the Germans, is a large bunker now covered in ivy, and close by is a small bunker, of the round roofed style more often used by the British, in the garden of a private house.

The site of Hollebeke Chateau, the scene of much action in 1914 during the first fighting for the ridge, is now farm land and no trace is evident. A farm house and yard stands at the former entrance to the grounds. The road junction here was named Kasteelhoek by the Germans after its Flemish name meaning the junction near the castle; in the angle formed by the roads was the site of a German gun battery, Batterie Mainz, and the large bunker for the battery still stands, the gothic script giving the name is still clearly readable on the inside wall. This is on private land and permission to visit should be requested from the farmhouse. Two more bunkers stood on the edge of the farm yard until the summer of 1997 when they were removed by heavy construction machinery.

The rebuilt village of Messines, with about 900 inhabitants, follows the same streets and layout as before it was destroyed. Messines Abbey was not resurrected but the church tower was modelled upon it. The church lighting was made by a German First World War soldier, Otto Meyer, and presented in 1967. By the side of the church is a panoramic view to the south, an orientation table gives information on what can be seen from here. The museum is worth a visit and contains some interesting artefacts and objects from the war, with much information on the New Zealanders.

Batterie Mainz near the site of Hollebeke Chateau. This battery was used by the Germans constantly, from before the 1917 Battle of Messines, during the battle, the 1918 spring offensive and the final advance, falling to the British at the end of September 1918.

British concrete bunker built close to the former German front line, close to the New Zealand Memorial Park. Built into the lee of the ridge after the Battle of Messines in 1917 it has a very thick roof (from door height to top) and strong reinforced walls on the German side, those facing the British are much thinner. A trench railway ran beside it. The very thick rear wall has received a direct hit from a heavy German shell and was damaged but remained intact (inset). The force of the explosion is evident on the inside face of the wall.

Wytschaete does not contain many signs or remnants from the fighting, a signpost on the main square gives directions for a 9km walk around some of the mine craters otherwise one could forget that this village has such a history. The site of The Hospice is now the village sports hall and soccer field. A walk in the woods will reveal some of the history as some shallow trench lines can be traced out and many shell holes are still there. Croonart Wood, which had been preserved, still contains many of the German trenches, some of which were maintained for seventy years, and a mine shaft and concrete bunkers, though some of these were brought here from other parts of the battlefield after the war.

BIBLIOGRAPHY AND FURTHER READING

Actions, operations, reports and anecdotes concerning the story of Messines Ridge (particularly the 1917 offensive and the mines) and its villages occur in fragmented form in many regimental and divisional histories, memoires and soldiers tales. Much of the earlier reading material is now out of print and available only through specialist dealers. Most volumes of the Official History of the War have been re-published by the Imperial War Museum/Battery Press and these provide much information. The following books contain part-histories and information on various aspects and all are either in print or generally easily available in public libraries.

Plumer The Soldiers General. G. Powell. pub. Leo Cooper,
Plumer of Messines. Gen C. Harington. pub. John Murray.
Orange Green and Khaki. T. Johnstone. pub. Gill and Macmillan.
Salient Points. T. Spagnoly and T. Smith. pub. Leo Cooper.
Hill 60. N. Cave. pub. Leo Cooper/Pen and Sword.
On The Western Front. J. Laffin. pub. Alan Sutton.
They Called It Passchendaele. L. Macdonald. pub. Papermac.
The Ypres Salient. M. Scott. pub. Gliddon Books.
Before Endeavours Fade. R. Coombs. pub. After The Battle.
Pill Boxes on the Western Front. P. Oldham. pub. Leo Cooper.
In Flanders Fields. L. Wolff. pub. Penguin.
Flanders Then and Now. J. Giles. pub. After The Battle.
Tunnellers. W. Grieve and B. Newman. pub. Naval and Military.
The War Underground. A. Barrie. pub. T. Donovan.
The Wet Flanders Plain. H. Williamson. pub. Gliddon Books.
Battle Book of Ypres. B. Brice. pub. Spa Books.

Selective Index

BRITISH ARMY

Baluchis 15,16
Bhopal 15
Dragoon Guards 16
Ferozepore 15
Hussars 16
Queen's Bays 16
Royals 15
Wilde's Rifles 15
Divisions:
9th 114,117
11th 99,101,108,131,133
16th 74,89,127
19th 100,114,129
24th 99,101
25th 85,88,89
30th 122
31st 120
34th 118,119,138
36th 88
37th 108,137
41st 93,94,104,121
47th 96

Regiments:
Argyll and Sutherland Highlanders 119
Cambridgeshire 32
Cameron Highlanders 117
Cheshire 23,24,66,92,94
Connought Rangers 15
Dorset 131
Dublin 67
Duke of Wellington's 132
Gloucestershire 94
Gordon Highlanders 20,21
Honourable Artillery Company 34
Inniskilling Fusiliers 17,68,69,89
K.O.Y.L.I. 17
K.O.S.B. 17,118,119
K.R.R.C. 94,104
Lancashire Fusiliers 87
Leinster 74,91
Lincolnshire 19,117
London 17,18,19,97,98,120
Loyal North Lancashire 87,92,118,119
Manchester 106
Middlesex 118,121,122,138
Munster 89
North Staffordshire 54,94,116
Northumberland Fusiliers
19,21,22,32,44,52,117
Queen's Royal West Surrey 104
Royal Irish 35,38,84,87,88,89,90,91,132,138
Royal Fusiliers 44,51,95
Royal Scots 20,21,48
Royal Welch Fusiliers 54,69,109
Royal West Kents 98,105,121,138
Warwickshire 67,116,132,138

West Yorkshire 48
Wiltshire 89
Other British Units:
Royal Engineers
1st and 2nd Field Squadrons 14,18
153 Field Company 137
154 Field Company 132
171 Tunnelling Company 57
172 Tunnelling Company 44
520 Field Company 98
Royal Flying Corps 66
Royal Garrison Artillery 20,113
Royal Naval Air Service 66
**DOMINION AND COMMONWEALTH
UNITS**
3rd Australian Division 80
4th Australian Division 99
33rd Battalion 82
37th Battalion 100,101
38th Battalion 80
39th Battalion 80
40th Battalion 80
45th Battalion 101
47th Battalion 100,102,132
48th Battalion 132
50th Battalion 103,104
52nd Battalion 103
1st Australian Engineers 130
4th Australian Engineers 137
7th Australian Engineers 113
Tasmanians 110
1st and 2nd Canadian Divisions 38
4th Canadian Brigade 40
6th Canadian Brigade 49
1st Battalion 43
19th Battalion 40
25th Battalion 43
27th Battalion 51
28th Battalion 43
29th Battalion 43
PPCLI 38,44
1st NZ Rifle Brigade 82,86
2nd NZ Rifle Brigade 68,83
3rd NZ Rifle Brigade 83
1st Auckland Battalion 85
1st Canterbury Battalion 83
2nd Canterbury Battalion 84
1st Otago Battalion 83,84
2nd Otago Battalion 65,84
1st Rifle Battalion 83
3rd Rifle Battalion 83,84
4th Rifle Battalion 85
1st Wellington Battalion 85
Chinese Labour Corps 127